I0233901

finding Jesus

CHERYL SASAI ELLICOTT

finding
Jesus

Studies in the Book of John

SEEK & YOU SHALL FIND
BOOK ONE

SWEETWATER STILL PUBLISHING

VISIT SWEETWATER STILL PUBLISHING AT:
www.sweetwaterstill.com

Finding Jesus © 2021 by Cheryl Sasai Ellicott. All rights reserved. Cover and interior design by Sweetwater Still. No part of this publication may be reproduced, stored in a retrieval system or transmitted in any form or by any means, electronic, mechanical, photocopying, recording, or otherwise without the prior written permission of the copyright holder, except brief quotations used in a review.

All Scriptures NLT unless otherwise noted. *Holy Bible,* New Living Translation (NLT), copyright 1996, 2004, 2015 by Tyndale House Foundation. Used by permission of Tyndale House Publishers, Inc., Carol Stream, Illinois 60188. All rights reserved. GW stands for God's Word translation.

ISBN: 978-1-7356345-1-7
LCCN: 2021935499
Categories 1. Christian Living 2. Discipleship 3. Bible Study

Published by Sweetwater Still Publishing
56893 S. 695 Rd.
Colcord, Oklahoma

Printed in the United States of America
25 24 23 22 21 / 9 8 7 6 5 4 3 2

"You search the Scriptures because you think they give you eternal life. But the Scriptures point to me!"

— Jesus

CONTENTS

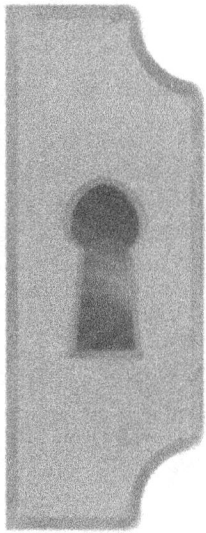

INTRODUCTION

Who is Jesus—and how can finding Him change your life in amazing and wonderful ways? This simple twelve-week study will answer those questions and teach you how to study and understand the Bible.

My journey to find Jesus began in 1986 when I began to wish there was more to life than just *what I could see.* At just nineteen years old, I was already weary of this world and my meaningless existence.

I remember standing in the dark, staring at the stars with a heavy heart. I whispered, "If there's anyone there, please answer me."

What happened next, and what I discovered, seemed too good to be true—*and it changed my life forever.*

Finding Jesus is the first book in the "SEEK & YOU SHALL FIND" series. I first taught this Bible study to house-churches in India. Because the message was given through a translator, it's intentionally brief and easy to follow.

I hope and pray this series of books will help you on your journey. If I can answer any questions or assist you further, please contact me through the book's publisher.

— *Cheryl Sasai Ellicott, 2021*

1

JESUS, WHERE ARE YOU?

You've decided to look for Jesus. **This is probably the best decision you've ever made.** But just deciding to look doesn't guarantee you'll succeed. These things will determine whether you succeed in finding Jesus or not:.

a.   where you search

b.   why you search

c.   how you react to what you find

SHOW ME YOUR JESUS!

Some people ask their society or culture to show them Jesus. But the Jesus your society or culture offers will always be their own creation—they invent a Jesus that agrees with their lifestyles.

1. Who does your society say Jesus is?

2. Who do you think Jesus is?

3. What will you do if you find out that you or your society are wrong?

Some people look inside of themselves, or look to their own visions and dreams hoping to find Jesus. Sure, the Spirit of Jesus can whisper into your heart. But your nature is the opposite of Jesus' nature, and your mind is an open court-yard where many spirits may stand up and speak. *Looking inside yourself* or believing every thought or spirit is a dangerous path with no guardrails!

4. What steps have you taken to listen and let the Spirit of God guide you?

5. What steps have you taken to guard yourself against lying spirits?

The Bible, **God's Word,** is your map; it leads to a firm, straight path—complete with guardrails. Once you're on this straight highway, staying within the borders created by the railings, the Spirit of Jesus can speak to you—and you'll have the tools you need to test every spirit.

READ 1 JOHN 4:1:

"Dear friends, do not believe everyone who claims to speak by the Spirit. You must test them to see if the spirit they have comes from God. For there are many false prophets in the world."

LOOK IN THE BIBLE!

If you don't have a Bible, make it your very strong goal and mission to have a Bible and to read it. If you don't have an easy-to-read Bible, find one.

When you study the Bible, it's important that it be written in your own language. Ignore people who tell you that only certain versions are inspired. Nonsense. Yes, some translations are *translated* more accurately than others, but in the beginning the most important thing is to read in a language that you understand! For English speaking people, this means to stay away from the *King James*—unless you actually speak "Early Modern English" in your daily life. But if you were born after AD 1700, you probably don't.

Once you have a Bible in your own language, you're on the right path. The *Holy Bible* is the inspired Word of God. It's more than a book—it's God's living, breathing, active Word; the same *Word* that created the heavens and the earth.

"By the word of the Lord the heavens were made, their starry host by the breath of his mouth." NIV

READ 2 TIMOTHY 3:15-17:

. . . "from infancy you have known the Holy Scriptures, which are able to make you wise for salvation through faith in Christ Jesus. 16 All Scripture is God-breathed and is useful for teaching, rebuking, correcting and training in righteousness, 17 so that the servant of God may be thoroughly equipped for every good work."

WHAT AM I REALLY LOOKING FOR?

Why do we read the Bible? We are searching for something. No matter what you're looking for, you will probably find it in the Scriptures. But if you're searching for your own opinion, idea or desire, you'll miss the main message. We must approach God's Word humbly, ready to accept whatever we find.

Many people read the Bible to find rules. There are rules—but if you're only looking for rules, you will find only rules.

Many are looking for knowledge. There is knowledge in the Bible—but if you search only for knowledge, you will find only knowledge. If you've already decided what you want to find, you'll ignore or miss the main message.

Jesus said, "You search the Scriptures because you think they give you eternal life. But the Scriptures point to me!"

Jesus was talking to religious people who searched the Scriptures because they wanted to live forever. Many people read the Bible for this reason. Whether you're seeking eternal life, heaven, or even abundant life here on earth—or just a reason to live—these are not bad reasons to read the Bible. The message of new life and eternal life are inside the Bible—but they're still the wrong things to look for, according to Jesus.

Read that last scripture again, but this time let's read some of the *context*. We find context by reading before and after the statement, to see who He's talking to and what He was talking about:

Jesus said, "And the Father who sent me has testified about me himself. You have never heard his voice or seen him face to face, 38 and you do not have his message in your hearts, because you do not believe me — the one he sent to you. 39 You search the Scriptures because you think they give you eternal life. But the Scriptures point to me! 40 Yet you refuse to come to me to receive this life." John 5:37-40

Jesus said, *"You search the Scriptures, looking for eternal life . . . but they point to me."* Read verse 40 one more time:

"... the Scriptures point to me! Yet you refuse to come to me to receive this life."

They refused to come to Jesus. When you search with an open heart, you'll see that the Scriptures are pointing you to Jesus! If you want life, you must come to Jesus. If you allow the Scriptures to speak to you and to guide you into their main message, you will come to Jesus—and all of these other things will be added to you as well.

WHICH GOD ARE WE TALKING ABOUT?

Before we can understand the things we're reading, we must know a couple of basic Bible truths that are *huge*.

> ONE: The God of the Bible declares that He is the only God.
>
> TWO: The Bible describes the one and only God as existing in three persons.

These concepts are beyond the focus of this study, so I won't explain them fully. But if you want to explore God's claims that *He is the only God*, start with these verses:

Isa. 44:6, Deut. 4:35, 1 Kings 8:60, James 2:19, 1 Timothy 2:5-6, Isa. 43:11, 1 Chr. 17:20, Isa. 46:9, 1 Cor. 8:6. And to briefly see God's claims of *existing in three persons*, start with these verses: Matt. 28:19, John 14:16-17, 26, 15:26, Acts 20:28, 1 Pet. 1:2, Col. 1:15-17, 2:9, 1 John 5:7-8.

Many other verses reveal the trinity, or triune nature of the one true God. For example: there are times when God has conversations with "Himself."

FIND JESUS; FIND EVERYTHING

If you search the Scriptures with an open heart, they will bring you to Jesus—and everything you need will be yours in and through Him.

READ LUKE 12:22-31:

Then, turning to his disciples, Jesus said:

"That is why I tell you not to worry about everyday life—whether you have enough food to eat or enough clothes to wear. 23 For life is more than food, and your body more than clothing. 24 Look at the ravens. They don't plant or harvest or store food in barns, for God feeds them. And you are far more valuable to him than any birds! 25 Can all your worries add a single moment to your life? 26 And if worry can't accomplish a little thing like that, what's the use of worrying over bigger things?

27 "Look at the lilies and how they grow. They don't work or make their clothing, yet Solomon in all his glory was not dressed as beautifully as they are. 28 And if God cares so wonderfully for flowers that are here today and thrown into the fire tomorrow, he will certainly care for you. Why do you have so little faith?

29 "And don't be concerned about what to eat and what to drink. Don't worry about such things. 30 These things dominate the thoughts of unbelievers all over the world, but your Father already knows your needs. 31 Seek the Kingdom of God above all else, and he will give you everything you need.'"

If we have Jesus and His kingdom, we have everything. God reveals Himself to us through Jesus, who Scripture calls "the Word of God."

READ JOHN 1:1-5:

"In the beginning the Word already existed. The Word was with God, and the Word was God. 2 He existed in the beginning with God. 3 God created everything through him, and nothing was created except through him. 4 The Word gave life to everything that was created, and his life brought light to everyone. 5 The light shines in the darkness, and the darkness can never extinguish it."

NOW READ VERSES 14-18:

"So the Word became human and made his home among us. He was full of unfailing love and faithfulness. And we have seen his glory, the glory of the Father's one and only Son.

15 John testified about him when he shouted to the crowds, 'This is the one I was talking about when I said, "Someone is coming after me who is far greater than I am, for he existed long before me.'"

16 From his abundance we have all received one gracious blessing after another. **17** For the law was given through Moses, but God's unfailing love and faithfulness came through Jesus Christ. **18** No one has ever seen God. But the unique One, who is himself God, is near to the Father's heart. He has revealed God to us."

6. According to John 1, who is "the Word of God"?

7. According to John 1:3, who is the Creator of the universe?

8. Which verses in John Chapter One declare that Jesus is God?

When you search the Scriptures, look for Jesus—and be ready to accept Him as He is! Don't expect Him to conform to your society's definition of *Jesus*. Approach God with a posture of humility, ready to change your mind or your opinions if you find out you've been wrong about Him or anything else.

Do this, and your search will be successful.

HOMEWORK:

Begin reading the book of John. Take notes and write down the things that you learn about Jesus.

Begin memorizing these verses:

Jeremiah 29:12-14: "'Then you will call on me and come and pray to me, and I will listen to you. 13 You will seek me and find me when you seek me with all your heart. 14 I will be found by you,' declares the Lord . . ." NIV

James 4:8: "Come near to God, and He will come near to you." NIV

Hebrews 11:6: "And without faith it is impossible to please God, because anyone who comes to him must believe that he exists and that he rewards those who earnestly seek him." NIV

2

STEP into
the LIGHT

Last week we began looking in
the Bible to find Jesus. We memorized Jeremiah 29:13, where God Almighty said: *"You
will seek Me and find Me when you search for
Me with all your heart."* (HCS) We also began
memorizing James 4:8: *"Come near to God,
and He will come near to you."* (NIV)

If those were the only Scriptures you had,
you might think that finding God is *up to
you.* It sounds like only noble-hearted people
who set out on this *noble* journey, looking for

God with all of their *noble* hearts, will find God. And if you're honest, you might admit that you're not entirely noble. But as you study more Scriptures, you'll get a broader understanding of what's involved in seeking and finding God.

We do not come to Jesus unless it's God's idea—He draws us to Christ (John 6:44). And He has given us this passage to tell us what sort of people he usually chooses:

READ 1 CORINTHIANS 1:26-29:

"**Remember, dear brothers and sisters, that few of you were wise in the world's eyes or powerful or wealthy when God called you. 27 Instead, God chose things the world considers foolish in order to shame those who think they are wise. And he chose things that are powerless to shame those who are powerful.**

28 God chose things despised by the world, things counted as nothing at all, and used them to bring to nothing what the world considers important. 29 As a result, no one can ever boast in the presence of God."

God chooses the foolish, powerless, and despised people. As a result, none of us can boast.

9. Considering all of your past actions, do you think God would call you noble, or foolish?

10. Why did you decide to begin looking for Jesus?

REVEALED *by the* LIGHT

"Afterward Jesus returned to Jerusalem for one of the Jewish holy days. 2 Inside the city, near the Sheep Gate, was the pool of Bethesda, with five covered porches. 3 Crowds of sick people—blind, lame, or paralyzed—lay on the porches. 5 One of the men lying there had been sick for thirty-eight years. 6 When Jesus saw him and knew he had been ill for a long time, he asked him, 'Would you like to get well?'

7 'I can't, sir,' the sick man said, 'for I have no one to put me into the pool when the water bubbles up. Someone else always gets there ahead of me.'

8 Jesus told him, 'Stand up, pick up your mat, and walk!'

9 Instantly, the man was healed! He rolled up his sleeping mat and began walking! But this miracle happened on the Sabbath, 10 so the Jewish leaders objected. They said to the man who was cured, 'You can't work on the Sabbath! The law doesn't allow you to carry that sleeping mat!'

11 But he replied, 'The man who healed me told me, "Pick up your mat and walk."'

12 'Who said such a thing as that?' they demanded.

13 The man didn't know, for Jesus had disappeared into the crowd. 14 But afterward Jesus found him in

the Temple and told him, 'Now you are well; so stop sinning, or something even worse may happen to you.' 15 Then the man went and told the Jewish leaders that it was Jesus who had healed him."

The man did not know who had healed him. He wasn't seeking Jesus; Jesus came looking for him. But he still hadn't had his sins forgiven; he was not reconciled with his Creator; he did not have eternal life. But then Jesus came and met him where he was (again). This time the man believed and came to know Christ; he was forgiven and made right with God.

In some places (in Scripture) we see that there were *conditions:* the people were required to have faith (and express it through action) before receiving anything. But this man didn't even know who Jesus was, and he received healing anyway. He was sick. So he went to the hot springs, or similar—down by the water, where other sick people were. He laid there for years, but it didn't help him. Finally, Jesus came looking for him, saw his need, and met his need. Jesus walked into a crowd of suffering people and healed just one. I believe that man was *the reason* that Jesus went there.

READ ROMANS 10:20:

"Isaiah spoke boldly for God, saying, 'I was found by people who were not looking for me. I showed myself to those who were not asking for me.'" NIV

Notice where the man was the next time Jesus found him. He'd been healed and now he could walk. So he got up and took steps toward finding God. When Jesus came looking for him again, the man was seeking God in the temple. But what did Jesus tell him?

READ JOHN 5:14:

"Jesus found him at the temple and said to him, 'See, you are well again. Stop sinning or something worse may happen to you.'"

Ouch!

11. What did Jesus say might happen to the man if he didn't stop sinning?

12. If you were told that your suffering was your own fault, how would you react?

JESUS OFFENDED ME!

Sometimes when people go looking for Jesus, they don't like what they find; it hurts their feelings. So they give up and go back. What do they find? They find themselves. And they are not the person they thought or hoped they were.

"But to those who don't believe: 'The stone that the builders rejected has become the cornerstone, a stone that people trip over, a large rock that people find offensive.' The people tripped over the word because they refused to believe it. Therefore, this is how they ended up." 1 Peter 2:7-8 GW

When people really find Jesus, He reveals their sin to them. They hear that their problems are their own fault. Many people are offended.

But Jesus is the light of the whole world. When you look for Jesus, you're coming close to a very bright light. You can't stand in this bright light without seeing things about yourself that you don't like. Everything that was hidden is exposed. You feel guilty. This doesn't make anyone feel happy. So some people choose not to believe what they're seeing, because they don't want to feel guilty. Instead, they try to get away from the light. They stop looking for Jesus, and they go back the way they came.

READ JOHN 12:46:

Jesus said, "I have come as a light to shine in this dark world, so that all who put their trust in me will no longer remain in the dark."

Many people become angry when they hear the name of Jesus—just hearing his name makes them feel exposed by the light. Even coming close to a Christian can remind them that they're sinners. When a believer walks into the room, the Spirit of Jesus walks in with them—because they have Christ's Spirit in them. Consider this passage:

READ 2 CORINTHIANS 2:14B-16A:

"Now he uses us to spread the knowledge of Christ everywhere, like a sweet perfume. 15 Our lives are a Christ-like fragrance rising up to God. But this fragrance is perceived differently by those who are being

saved and by those who are perishing. 16 To those who are perishing, we are a dreadful smell of death and doom. But to those who are being saved, we are a life-giving perfume."

After people reject Jesus, even His name becomes an offense to them. And His followers are a dreadful smell of death and doom.

But many people who rejected Jesus are still religious. When people stop looking for Jesus, some choose religion instead. They don't want to get too close to God, and they don't want Him to come too near to them. They don't want to seek Him with all of their hearts. But they want religion! Some of them want a lot of religion, so they can feel like they're good people.

NOTHING but a SINNER?

Why do we need a savior? Many people search the Scriptures looking for knowledge and rules. They want to keep some rules so they can feel good and worthy. But if we honestly search the Bible for rules, the knowledge we get is this:

I am not worthy. I am guilty. No matter how hard I try, I'll never earn the right to stand in God's presence.

JAMES 2:10 SAYS:

"For the person who keeps all of the laws except one is as guilty as a person who has broken all of God's laws."

What does this say? And what does it mean? If I am almost perfect and keep almost all of God's laws, almost all of the time, then I am no better than the person who breaks all of them all the time? Yes. That is what the Bible says.

13. Have you ever broken any of God's laws?

14. How does James 2:10 make you feel about yourself?

LET'S TURN TO ROMANS 3:20:

"For no one can ever be made right with God by doing what the law commands. The law simply shows us how sinful we are."

(Keep a bookmark here because we will return to Romans Chapter Three later.) So if we go looking for Jesus—with all of our hearts—what will we find? *Bad news.* We'll find out how sinful we are.

But if we do not turn away, and if we do not run away, and if we keep seeking Jesus, we can find more than this. When we see our sinfulness and accept it as truth, we are agreeing with God. We're saying:

Yes, Lord, I'm lost. Yes, Lord, I'm a sinner. I deserve death. I need a Savior!

If we keep seeking Him like this, we will find Him.

I NEED FORGIVENESS!

When we look for Jesus, we will find God's son; the Messiah, the Savior of the world; God in flesh. John 1:3 calls Jesus *the Creator of all things.* And who is the Creator? God.

LET'S READ ROMANS 3:22-25:

"We are made right with God by placing our faith in Jesus Christ. And this is true for everyone who believes, no matter who we are. 23 For everyone has sinned; we all fall short of God's glorious standard."

All people haven sinned. Every person falls short of God's requirements—His glorious standard. We all stand condemned already, with no hope of redeeming ourselves.

NOW READ VERSES 24-25:

24 "Yet God, in his grace, freely makes us right in his sight. He did this through Christ Jesus when he freed us from the penalty for our sins. 25 For God presented Jesus as the sacrifice for sin. People are made right with God when they believe that Jesus sacrificed his life, shedding his blood."

ROMANS 10:9-10 SAYS:

"If you openly declare that Jesus is Lord and believe in your heart that God raised him from the dead, you will be saved. 10 For it is by believing in your heart that you are made right with God, and it is by openly declaring your faith that you are saved."

15. How are we made right with God, according to Romans 3:22-25 and 10:9-10 ?

16. Do you believe you have been made right with God? Explain.

LET'S FINISH WITH 1 JOHN 1:5-9:

"This is the message we heard from Jesus and now declare to you: God is light, and there is no darkness in him at all. 6 So we are lying if we say we have fellowship with God but go on living in spiritual darkness; we are not practicing the truth. 7 But if we are living in the light, as God is in the light, then we have fellowship with each other, and the blood of Jesus, his Son, cleanses us from all sin. 8 If we claim we have no sin, we are only fooling ourselves and not living in the truth. 9 But if we confess our sins to him, he is faithful and just to forgive us our sins and to cleanse us from all wickedness."

When you draw near to God, He will draw near to you. When you seek Him with all of your heart, you will find Him—but you will find the bright light of God's law shining on you. You will see your sinfulness. You will either run away, or you will repent.

If you admit you are a sinner, and you confess your sins to Jesus, He will forgive you through His finished work on the cross.

This is the beginning of a brand new life. Ask Jesus to fill you with His Holy Spirit. Ask Him to change you, so that you can continue to walk in His light without shame. And any time He shows you your sin, repent right away—ask Jesus to forgive you and to cleanse you and make you pure.

HOMEWORK:

If you haven't finished reading the book of John, please continue and write down the things you learn about Jesus. If you finished John, begin the book of Matthew for the same true story told by a different eye-witness.

PRACTICE THESE MEMORY VERSES:

Romans 3:23-24: . . . "for all have sinned and fall short of the glory of God, 24 and all are justified freely by his grace through the redemption that came by Christ Jesus." NIV

Romans 6:22-23: "But now that you have been set free from sin and have become slaves of God, the benefit you reap leads to holiness, and the result is eternal life. 23 For the wages of sin is death, but the gift of God is eternal life in Christ Jesus our Lord." NIV

1 John 1:7: "But if we walk in the light, as he is in the light, we have fellowship with one another, and the blood of Jesus, his Son, purifies us from all sin."

3

AT the CROSSROADS

When we find Jesus, will we accept Him completely? Or will we only accept the things about Him that we feel comfortable with? The Bible teaches that our God is the Creator of all things, and He exists in three persons: God the Father, Jesus the Son, and the Holy Spirit.

John Chapter One tells us that Jesus is the Creator. At one point His followers had just watched Him walk on water and feed thousands of people miraculously. His miracles proved that He was the *Messiah* (or Savior).

But then He said something that offended a lot of people, and many of them left.

READ JOHN 6:68:

"Jesus turned to the Twelve and asked, 'Are you also going to leave?'

Simon Peter replied, 'Lord, to whom would we go? You alone have the words that give eternal life. We believe, and we know you are the Holy One of God.'"

BEWARE of the WIDE PATH

Many people *pray* and *do good works.* They are very religious; many *call themselves Christians* and *read the Bible.* They might even argue about who knows more scriptures! They are often in church and even become leaders in the church.

But they are on a wide road to hell.

READ MATTHEW 7:13-14:

Jesus said, "You can enter God's Kingdom only through the narrow gate. The highway to hell is broad, and its gate is wide for the many who choose that way. 14 But the gateway to life is very narrow and the road is difficult, and only a few ever find it."

The world is filled with religious people traveling on religious pathways. But Jesus says only a few will find the highway to eternal life. *Why?* They refuse to go through the narrow gate that Jesus provides.

The Bible declares that we were born with a sinful nature; it controls us through our feelings. Having a set of religious beliefs and rules, and then trying hard to keep them, doesn't change our sinful core. It doesn't set us free from the power of our nature.

People who are only religious are like the Pharisees, who were responsible for crucifying Jesus. Consider what Jesus said to the most religious people of His day:

LUKE 22:52-53:

"Then Jesus said to the chief priests and officers of the temple and elders who had come against Him, 'Have you come out with swords and clubs as you would against a robber? 53 While I was with you daily in the temple, you did not lay hands on Me; but this hour and the power of darkness are yours.'"

If extremely religious people can still be under the power of darkness, still on the wide road to hell, then who can be saved? What is this narrow path?

17. If God asks you, "Why should I let you into Heaven?" what will you answer?

18. If you obey a set of religious beliefs and rules, how do you know your list is the same list God judges by?

Many people agree that Jesus Christ is the only way to Heaven. But true acceptance of Jesus always results in a changed heart and changed life. If your life hasn't changed, your heart hasn't changed because you haven't truly accepted Him yet.

Some people who call themselves Christians use the "I'm just a sinner saved by grace" excuse when the Holy Spirit convicts them of sin. They make excuses when God reveals their sin and asks them to walk in the light. But the Bible declares that those who walk in darkness are still controlled by their fallen nature. And if they're still under the power of darkness; they're still on the wide road to hell, no matter how religious they are.

> **Why does genuine faith in Jesus result in changed lives? Because when we come to faith in Jesus, His righteous, all-powerful Spirit comes to live inside of our bodies.**

WHO'S IN CONTROL?

Whether you're on the *wide path* or the *narrow path* is all a matter of control. Who controls your actions and thoughts? All cultures have some understanding of what happens when an evil foreign spirit enters into a person's body: it seizes control. If an evil spirit, or the devil, enters your body and takes control, then wickedness, suffering and great harm are the results.

But what would happen if a perfect, holy, loving Spirit moved into your body?

ROMANS 8:9 SAYS:

"...the Spirit of God dwells in you. Anyone who does not have the Spirit of Christ does not belong to him."

DON'T WALK ALONE!

As we seek Jesus, we learn that we're sinners. We learn that we need forgiveness.

If we believe that Jesus died on the cross, to pay a debt that we owed, then we must ask Him to forgive our sins. He will cleanse us, by the blood that he shed. And we receive His righteousness.

But now our faith is proven to be real when we turn away from wickedness and walk in the light. Not when we *try to turn away*, but when we actually succeed!

Why is success the proof? Anyone who tries in their own power (without the Spirit of Jesus controlling them) will fail.

We are not capable of walking in the light without the Spirit of Light. We need the Holy Spirit of Jesus living inside of our bodies. That's the only way we can break free from the power of our fallen nature. And Romans 8:9 says that we do not belong to Christ if we don't have His Spirit dwelling inside of us.

To put this into perspective, imagine that you wanted to act like the devil—not only on the outside, but on the inside too. Without some help from an evil force, you'd only be a pretender.

You might put on a pretty good show, on the outside—but your inner man wouldn't really change. However, because you have a sinful nature you could probably come up with some very wicked behavior. But your act would not compare with the level of depravity and horror you'll experience if the devil actually moves into your body and controls you.

The same is true for a person who wants to act like Jesus. Without the actual Holy Spirit of Jesus coming into your body, you can only be a pretender—or as the Bible puts it, a hypocrite.

But there is one difference, and it's worth mentioning: the devil (or an evil spirit) is evil, therefore they seize control and destroy the person they inhabit. The Holy Spirit, on the other hand, is perfect, righteous, and good. The Holy Spirit of Jesus does not seize control. He will give you the supernatural power to do the impossible only when you want Him to, and the results will bring healing, joy, and new life.

In John 16:7 Jesus said that He was returning to the Father, and then He would send His Holy Spirit, "the helper," to live inside of us:

> **"I tell you the truth: it is to your advantage that I go away, for if I do not go away, the Helper will not come to you. But if I go, I will send him to you."**

19. What types of behavior do you expect to see from a demon–possessed person?
20. What actions do you expect to see from a person who has God's Holy Spirit in them?

JESUS PURCHASED ME

You might hear people say that Jesus died on the cross to pay the price for your sins. By this unclear statement, you might think he died to buy *your sins*. This is false. He doesn't want to buy your sins.

He died to pay the penalty for your sins, but he was not purchasing *your sins*. He was purchasing *you*.

"Don't you realize that your body is the temple of the Holy Spirit, who lives in you and was given to you by God? You do not belong to yourself, 20 for God bought you with a high price. So you must honor God with your body."

God bought you with a high price—that price was the life and blood of His Son, Jesus. Therefore, you do not belong to yourself anymore. You've received new life. Now Jesus plans to use your body for good.

READ JOHN 15:1-3:

Jesus said, "I am the true vine, and my Father is the gardener. 2 He cuts off every branch in me that bears no fruit, while every branch that does bear fruit he prunes so that it will be even more fruitful. 3 You are already clean because of the word I have spoken to you."

We became clean when we believed in Jesus and asked Him to forgive our sins. He washed us clean by His sacrifice on the cross, by his blood. And now he wants to grow His fruit in our lives!

NOW READ VERSES 4-5:

"Remain in me, as I also remain in you. No branch can bear fruit by itself; it must remain in the vine. Neither can you bear fruit unless you remain in me. 5 I am the vine; you are the branches. If you remain in me and I

in you, you will bear much fruit; apart from me you can do nothing."

JESUS LIVES INSIDE ME

After purchasing us for God, Jesus has plans to live inside of us—we are His temple. And He plans to grow His fruit inside of us. Jesus said we must remain in Him and He must remain in us. He promises we will bear much fruit if we remain in Him and He stays in us.

If this doesn't make sense, you may need to ask Jesus to fill you with His Holy Spirit. Keep your bookmark in John 15.

LET'S READ LUKE 11:11-13:

Jesus said, "Which of you fathers, if your son asks for a fish, will give him a snake instead? 12 Or if he asks for an egg, will give him a scorpion? 13 If you then, though you are evil, know how to give good gifts to your children, how much more will your Father in heaven give the Holy Spirit to those who ask him!"

It is not hard to receive the Holy Spirit of Jesus. Just ask! If needed, do that now . . .

RETURN TO JOHN 15. READ VERSES 6-8:

Jesus said, "If you do not remain in me, you are like a branch that is thrown away and withers; such branches are picked up, thrown into the fire and burned. 7 If

you remain in me and my words remain in you, ask whatever you wish, and it will be done for you. 8 This is to my Father's glory, that you bear much fruit, showing yourselves to be my disciples."

If we remain in Jesus and His Spirit remains in us, we will grow much fruit. This fruit is God's character. We will do things that God would do. Because Jesus is God, this means we will act like Jesus to the extent that we allow Him to control us. However, there will be a constant battle; since the fall of man in the Garden of Eden, all people are born with a sinful nature. With each decision, we must choose to deny our nature and yield to the Spirit of Jesus. (You can read about this in Genesis Chapter Three.)

READ GALATIANS 5:19-21:

"When you follow the desires of your sinful nature, the results are very clear: sexual immorality, impurity, lustful pleasures, 20 idolatry, sorcery, hostility, quarreling, jealousy, outbursts of anger, selfish ambition, dissension, division, 21 envy, drunkenness, wild parties, and other sins like these. Let me tell you again, as I have before, that anyone living that sort of life will not inherit the Kingdom of God."

Those verses describe the nature all people are born with. God is love; His nature is 100% unselfish. But men and women are born with selfish, sinful natures. Without the help of God's Spirit, even our good works are stained and polluted by a proud, selfish nature that wants to be first and best, that wants to be honored and praised etc.

"But the Holy Spirit produces this kind of fruit in our lives: love, joy, peace, patience, kindness, goodness, faithfulness, 23 gentleness, and self-control. There is no law against these things! 24 Those who belong to Christ Jesus have nailed the passions and desires of their sinful nature to his cross and crucified them there. 25 Since we are living by the Spirit, let us follow the Spirit's leading in every part of our lives."

LET the SPIRIT of JESUS LEAD

Our old sinful nature will still exist. But now, with the help of God's Holy Spirit, we can escape its control. We can now say No! to our selfish feelings and desires. As we practice this, Jesus grows His fruit—love—in our lives. Remember: unlike an evil spirit, the Spirit of Jesus continues to allow us to choose—even though He owns us and has the right and the power to control us.

Let's return to John 15:4-5:

Jesus said, "Remain in me, as I also remain in you. No branch can bear fruit by itself; it must remain in the vine. Neither can you bear fruit unless you remain in me. 5 I am the vine; you are the branches. If you remain in me and I in you, you will bear much fruit; apart from me you can do nothing."

This narrow path is the only way to life. But to walk this path, Jesus said we must stay in Him and He must stay in us. As believers, we are now living with two natures inside of us: we have "the flesh" (our old sinful nature), and we have the perfect, loving Holy Spirit of Jesus. Our body's feelings will often come from the body, from the old sinful nature.

When a person is separated from the Holy Spirit, they can only choose to obey their feelings or their own understanding. But when we have the Spirit of Jesus, we can choose to ignore our selfish feelings, ignore our own reasoning, and obey God's nature. This is called *walking by faith.*

It takes faith to go against what your body and mind are telling you!

As we walk this narrow path, we decide every moment to follow and obey His nature—especially when we come to a crossroads where our feelings go one way and the Spirit of Jesus goes the other. Here's an illustration of what that looks like:

READ ROMANS 13:8-14:

"Owe nothing to anyone—except for your obligation to love one another. If you love your neighbor, you will fulfill the requirements of God's law. 9 For the commandments say, 'You must not commit adultery. You must not murder. You must not steal. You must not covet.' These—and other such commandments— are summed up in this one commandment: 'Love your neighbor as yourself.' 10 Love does no wrong to others, so love fulfills the requirements of God's law.

11 This is all the more urgent, for you know how late it is; time is running out. Wake up, for our salvation is nearer now than when we first believed. **12** The night is almost gone; the day of salvation will soon be here. So remove your dark deeds like dirty clothes, and put on the shining armor of right living.

13 Because we belong to the day, we must live decent lives for all to see. Don't participate in the darkness of wild parties and drunkenness, or in sexual promiscuity and immoral living, or in quarreling and jealousy. **14** Instead, clothe yourself with the presence of the Lord Jesus Christ. And don't let yourself think about ways to indulge your evil desires."

Following the narrow path, walking in the light, means to walk in *sacrificial love*. It means to agree with God, by the supernatural power of His Holy Spirit. When my nature has a different opinion, I must agree with God's nature and ask Him to help me stay in step with His Spirit.

> 21. According to Galatians 5:19–21, what traits or actions come from human nature?
> 22. According to Galatians 5:22–25, what traits or actions are produced by the Holy Spirit?

HOMEWORK:

If you have finished reading the entire book of John, read the book of Matthew. If you have finished that also, read the book of Mark. These books tell the same true story, but from different eye-witnesses.

PRACTICE THESE MEMORY VERSES:

Hebrews 9:22: "In fact, the law requires that nearly everything be cleansed with blood, and without the shedding of blood there is no forgiveness." NIV

Romans 6:11-12: "In the same way, count yourselves dead to sin but alive to God in Christ Jesus. 12 Therefore do not let sin reign in your mortal body so that you obey its evil desires." NIV

Romans 8:8-9: "Those who are in the realm of the flesh cannot please God. 9 You, however, are not in the realm of the flesh but are in the realm of the Spirit, if indeed the Spirit of God lives in you. And if anyone does not have the Spirit of Christ, they do not belong to Christ." NIV

4

CAN YOU TRUST HIM?

We read the Bible looking for **Jesus**, and we look for Jesus because He is the light of the world and He is the only way to heaven.

John 8:12: "Again Jesus spoke to them, saying, 'I am the light of the world. Whoever follows me will not walk in darkness, but will have the light of life.'"

John 14:6: "Jesus told him, 'I am the way, the truth, and the life. No one can come to the Father except through me.'"

Here are some things we've learned:

> A. If we seek God with all of our hearts, we will find Him. (Jeremiah 29:13-14)
>
> B. When we draw near to God, He will come near to us. (James 4:8)
>
> C. But then we will be exposed. We will come into the LIGHT. (John 12:46)
>
> D. Jesus wants to live inside of us; we are His temple. (1 Corinthians 6:19)
>
> E. Jesus bought us with His blood; this is why we obey. (1 Corinthians 6:20)
>
> F. If the Spirit of Christ doesn't live in us, we are not His people. (Romans 8:9)

DID YOU TAKE the NARROW PATH?

When we come to (the real, true, biblical) Jesus, He reveals our sin to us. We must not run away from the light. We must agree with Him and confess our sins to Him.

If we confess our sins, He'll forgive and cleanse us.

But some people will run away from Jesus because they love darkness. And if you begin to walk in the light, people who love darkness will feel uncomfortable around you too. Sadly, as we walk this narrow path, we might lose friends. People who used to love us will push us away because the Spirit of Jesus inside of us is too bright.

JOHN 3:19:

"This is the judgment, that the Light has come into the world, and men loved the darkness rather than the Light, for their deeds were evil."

1 JOHN 1:9:

"But if we confess our sins to him, he is faithful and just to forgive us our sins and to cleanse us from all wickedness."

YOU'RE NOT WALKING ALONE!

You might lose old friends or even family members, but you will gain new ones. When you put your trust in Jesus, you become a child of God—you have new family all over the world. Everyone who is truly *in Christ* is now your brother or sister.

It's God's will that we find true believers and remain in fellowship with them, studying the Bible together and praying for each other. The Bible is *God's Word;* it's your roadmap as you travel this new path. And God's Word commands us to love other believers, deeply from our hearts, and to encourage one another daily. Your new family is very real. If you have not yet met them, ask Jesus to bring you together.

READ 1 PETER 1:21-22:

"Through Christ you have come to trust in God. And you have placed your faith and hope in God because he raised Christ from the dead and gave him great glory. 22 You were cleansed from your sins when you obeyed the truth, so now you must show sincere love to each other as brothers and sisters. Love each other deeply with all your heart."

READ HEBREWS 10:24-25:

"Let us think of ways to motivate one another to acts of love and good works. 25 And let us not neglect our meeting together, as some people do, but encourage one another, especially now that the day of his return is drawing near."

But that's not all—you also have God's Holy Spirit now. When you *ask Him,* Jesus will send His Holy Spirit to live inside of you and to empower you in your new life.

ASK HIM to CARRY YOU ALONG

Jesus doesn't expect you to use your own strength to follow Him. You cannot do this alone. You need the power of God's Holy Spirit—and He is willing and waiting to carry you along His path by the power of His Spirit within you.

He's just waiting for you to ask.

Any time our own desires are the opposite of God's will (as revealed in His Word), we must agree with God. We must turn around, turn away, repent, and follow God's plan.

His Holy Spirit gives us the power and desire to obey. (Romans 8:13, Philippians 2:13)

PHILIPPIANS 2:13:

"God is always at work in you to make you willing and able to obey his own purpose." GNB

LUKE 11:13:

"So if you sinful people know how to give good gifts to your children, how much more will your heavenly Father give the Holy Spirit to those who ask him."

His Holy Spirit will reveal God's will to us. He reveals His will through His Word, the Bible. His Holy Spirit will give us the power to obey what we read there as we surrender to Him, moment by moment in each decision.

JOHN 14:15-17:

Jesus said, "If you love me, obey my commandments. 16 And I will ask the Father, and he will give you another Advocate, who will never leave you. 17 He is the Holy Spirit, who leads into all truth. The world cannot receive him, because it isn't looking for him and doesn't recognize him. But you know him, because he lives with you now and later will be in you."

23. Where do believers get the power to obey God's Word and His will?

24. Has God's Word ever shown you that you were *out of God's will?* How did you respond?

HOW to STUDY YOUR ROADMAP

The safest ways to study the Bible are "expository" and "verse by verse." Expository comes from the verb *exposit* which is related to the word *expose.* To exposit means to expound—to explain by presenting careful and often elaborate detail. So expository teaching will search deeply into verses to find the fullest meaning.

And the most logical way to teach in an expository manner is to carefully explore the entire paragraph, then the chapter, and then the book—in other words, *verse by verse.*

By studying this way, we guard against misunderstandings that are common when people take things "out of context."

A sentence can easily be misunderstood when it is removed from the paragraph it belongs in. And a paragraph makes less sense when removed from the chapter and book to which it belongs.

The safest way to understand what is being said is to listen carefully to the entire message.

The Bible was not written in free-standing sentences but rather as coherent and fully-formed messages (in book or letter form) containing many sentences that support and explain each other.

LET'S TRY IT OUT!

This week we will begin to read the book of John together. We will study verse by verse, with a somewhat expository method—this Bible study is brief, so we will not exposit or expound exhaustively. But we will explore other parts of the Bible that talk about the same thing.

LET'S START IN JOHN CHAPTER 1, VERSES 1-2:

"In the beginning the Word already existed. The Word was with God, and the Word was God. 2 He existed in the beginning with God."

What does this say, and what could it mean? It says that this character named *the Word* is God. He has always existed. He is God, and yet He was *with God.* Already we're seeing a very complex character, one that is said to be "with" Himself.

NOW READ VERSE 3:

"God created everything through him, and nothing was created except through him."

This character, *the Word,* is the Creator of all things. He created everything. Nothing at all was created except through His hand.

READ VERSES 4 AND 5:

"The Word gave life to everything that was created, and his life brought light to everyone. 5 The light shines in the darkness, and the darkness can never extinguish it."

Life is in *the Word*—He is the one who gave life to everything that has life. He is the one and only life-giver. He is the light and He shines in the darkness. The darkness has no power over Him.

READ VERSES 6-9:

"God sent a man, John the Baptist, 7 to tell about the light so that everyone might believe because of his testimony. 8 John himself was not the light; he was simply a witness to tell about the light. 9 The one who is the true light, who gives light to everyone, was coming into the world."

God chose a man named John and sent him to tell people that *the light* was coming. John was announcing His coming and witnessing about this light, who is also called *the Word.*

READ VERSES 10-13:

"He came into the very world he created, but the world didn't recognize him. 11 He came to his own

people, and even they rejected him. 12 But to all who believed him and accepted him, he gave the right to become children of God. 13 They are reborn—not with a physical birth resulting from human passion or plan, but a birth that comes from God."

The Word came to the people He had created and to the nation He had chosen as His own, but most of them didn't realize their Savior had come. That is still true today. But if you believe, you become God's child. You are born again. Then you begin your journey, walking with Him and getting to know Him.

READ VERSE 14:

"So the Word became human and made his home among us. He was full of unfailing love and faithfulness. And we have seen his glory, the glory of the Father's one and only Son."

Now we see that this entire section of Scripture is talking about Jesus! He is the character called *the Word.* By this section of Scripture alone, we see that Jesus is God; He is the giver of life, He is the light of the world, and He is the Creator of all things.

We also see that His character is unfailing love and faithfulness, and that He is the only Son of God—while also being God Himself. As we mentioned earlier, He's the most complex character you will ever meet. And yes, you can meet Him. We will learn through more study of the Scriptures that you can know Jesus, personally. Not through the priest, the prophet or the preacher, but through His Spirit.

You can know Jesus through His Holy Word and His Spirit living inside of you.

Will you study His Word? Have you invited his Spirit to live inside of your body? If not, you can do that now!

HOMEWORK:

If you've finished reading the books of John, Matthew and Mark, now read the book of Luke. This tells the same story from yet another eyewitness.

PRACTICE THESE MEMORY VERSES:

John 1:1: "In the beginning was the Word, and the Word was with God, and the Word was God." NIV

John 1:14: "The Word became flesh and made his dwelling among us. We have seen his glory, the glory of the one and only Son, who came from the Father, full of grace and truth." NIV

John 14:6: "Jesus answered, 'I am the way and the truth and the life. No one comes to the Father except through me.'" NIV

5

LOVE
ILLUSTRATED

We've been studying the Scriptures to find Jesus—and we found that He is very complex:

Jesus is God, the Creator of all things. But He's also said to be *with God* and called *the Son of God.*

Jesus is unlike any other character. In fact, He is the only God—there is no other.

Genesis 1:1, 26a: "In the beginning God created the heavens and the earth . . . Then God said, 'Let us make human beings in our image, to be like us . . .'"

Deuteronomy 4:35, 39: "He showed you these things so you would know that the LORD is God and there is no other . . . So remember this and keep it firmly in mind: The LORD is God both in heaven and on earth, and there is no other."

Isaiah 44:6, 8: "This is what the LORD says — Israel's King and Redeemer, the LORD of Heaven's Armies: 'I am the First and the Last; there is no other God . . . Do not tremble; do not be afraid. Did I not proclaim my purposes for you long ago? You are my witnesses — is there any other God? No! There is no other Rock — not one!'"

Isaiah 45:18: "For thus says the Lord, who created the heavens (he is God!), who formed the earth and made it (he established it; he did not create it empty, he formed it to be inhabited!): 'I am the Lord, and there is no other.'"

1 Timothy 2:5-6a: "For, there is one God and one Mediator who can reconcile God and humanity — the man Christ Jesus. 6 He gave his life to purchase freedom for everyone . . ."

As we study the entire Bible, we see these truths explained many times, in great detail.

Jesus is God, the Creator of all things, and there is no other God. There are other so-called *gods*, but they're false. If they have any power at all, it's because they're demons (evil spirits).

Our world contains many evil spirits—the Bible shows that they were angels (created by God) who rebelled against God and were thrown out of heaven. Now they are God's enemies, and they are your enemies. But remember: they were created by God! Even the devil is a created being; he is not all-powerful. The devil and the other evil spirits are weak compared to our God, Jesus.

ONE GOD in THREE PERSONS

Our God is all-powerful, and He has existed forever; He was not created. The Bible clearly shows that He is one God, but He consists of three persons:

God the Father,
Jesus the Son,
and the Holy Spirit.

LET'S READ ISAIAH 9:6:

"For a child is born to us, a son is given to us. The government will rest on his shoulders. And he will be called: Wonderful Counselor, Mighty God, Everlasting Father, Prince of Peace."

The prophet Isaiah said that a child would be born, and He'd be the Everlasting Father, and Mighty God.

As we have seen, John Chapter One told us that Jesus is that child. Jesus is the Creator of all things who came to earth as a baby. So the prophet Isaiah was talking about Jesus when he announced the coming of the Creator (the author of life) hundreds of years before His birth. Other prophets also foretold that the Creator would come to die on a cross and then be raised from death.

READ ACTS 3:15:15:

"You killed the author of life, but God raised him from the dead. And we are witnesses of this fact!"

If anyone tries to tell you that Jesus is not God in the flesh, don't listen to them. Jesus said, **"If you do not believe that I am He, you will die in your sins."** The Bible declares that Jesus is the only Savior. If you want to study more verses that speak of the deity of Christ, look at these:

John 1:1, 14, 18, John 5:18, John 8:22-24, 57-58, John 10:30, 33, John 17:21, 1 Corinthians 8:6, Philippians 2:5-6, Colossians 2:9-10, Romans 10:13, 1 John 5:20, Revelation 1:17-18, Revelation 2:8.

25. Who do you believe Jesus is?

26. What facts or experiences are your beliefs founded on?

JESUS is the STAIRWAY BETWEEN HEAVEN and EARTH

If you want to ascend or descend, you need something like a ladder or a stairway. The Bible tells us that Jesus is the *only way* to reach God. In the following scriptures Jesus is described as the Son of God, the King of Israel—and the stairway between heaven and earth!

READ JOHN 1:49-51:

"Then Nathanael exclaimed, 'Rabbi, you are the Son of God—the King of Israel!'

50 Jesus asked him, 'Do you believe this just because I told you I had seen you under the fig tree? You will see greater things than this.' 51 Then he said, 'I tell you the truth, you will all see heaven open and the angels of God going up and down on the Son of Man, the one who is the stairway between heaven and earth.'"

Last week we began studying verse by verse through the book of John. We're going to continue exploring this book slowly. We're still in John Chapter One. Let's begin by reading verse 14:

READ JOHN 1:14:

"So the Word became human and made his home among us. He was full of unfailing love and faithfulness. And we have seen his glory, the glory of the Father's one and only Son."

Last week, in verses 1-4, we saw that *the Word* was God the Creator. And we saw that *the Word* became a human and lived with us. This was clearly talking about Jesus; He is the only God who became human and lived among us.

NOW READ VERSES 15-17:

"John testified about him when he shouted to the crowds, 'This is the one I was talking about when I said, "Someone is coming after me who is far greater than I am, for he existed long before me." 16 From his abundance we have all received one gracious blessing after another. 17 For the law was given through Moses, but God's unfailing love and faithfulness came through Jesus Christ.'"

What came to us through Jesus? God's unfailing love and faithfulness. And how did God's love and faithfulness come to us through Jesus? Well, He healed people—that's loving. But was that the epitome of His love? No, this verse speaks of a more complete revelation of God's love. He fed hungry people—that's loving. Was that God's unfailing love and faithfulness coming to us through Jesus? No, I still think He's speaking of something more, a love greater than just healing and food. You can be healed in your body and still go to hell. You can eat and have a full stomach, and you can still go to hell. So how exactly did the fullness of God's unfailing love come to us through Jesus?

The fullness of God's unfailing love came to us through the cross.

THE CROSS *is* GOD'S LOVE
ILLUSTRATED

Scripture says that you and I owe a sin debt that we cannot pay. Jesus gave God's love to us by taking our place on the cross, in death, in shedding His blood to pay for our sin.

LET'S READ JOHN 1:18:

"No one has ever seen God. But the unique One, who is himself God, is near to the Father's heart. He has revealed God to us."

Jesus reveals God to us, because Jesus is God who came to us in human form. And what does Jesus show us about God? He shows us that God is love— the type of love that would die for you when you are His enemy who does not deserve His love.

LET'S READ ROMANS 3:9B-12:

". . . all people, whether Jews or Gentiles, are under the power of sin. 10 As the Scriptures say, 'No one is righteous—not even one. 11 No one is truly wise; no one is seeking God. 12 All have turned away; all have become useless. No one does good, not a single one.'"

READ ROMANS 5:8:

"But God showed his great love for us by sending Christ to die for us while we were still sinners."

READ ROMANS 6:22-23:

"But now you are free from the power of sin and have become slaves of God. Now you do those things that lead to holiness and result in eternal life. 23 For the wages of sin is death, but the free gift of God is eternal life through Christ Jesus our Lord."

Jesus died on the cross because of our sin. But I want you to notice what Romans 6:22-23 reveals:

If you accept the sacrifice of Jesus (in your place), you are exchanging your old life (which results in death) and you are becoming slaves of God (which results in holiness and eternal life).

LET'S READ 1 JOHN 1:9:

"But if we confess our sins to him, he is faithful and just to forgive us our sins and to cleanse us from all wickedness."

NOW READ 1 JOHN 4:9-10:

"God showed how much he loved us by sending his one and only Son into the world so that we might have eternal life through him. 10 This is real love—not that we loved God, but that he loved us and sent his Son as a sacrifice to take away our sins."

God revealed His love through the cross.

READ ACTS 4:12:

"There is salvation in no one else! God has given no other name under heaven by which we must be saved."

27. According the John 1:18, what did Jesus reveal to us?

28, Why did Jesus have to die on the cross?

Jesus is God, the Creator of all things, and there is no other God — there are other so-called *gods*, but they are false. And our God is love. His love gave us a stairway to heaven.

The cross illustrates God's love.

Jesus is the stairway—through His death on the cross, He made the way for us to ascend to the Father.

HOMEWORK:

If you've finished reading the gospels of Matthew, Mark, Luke and John, now begin reading the book of Acts.

PRACTICE THESE MEMORY VERSES:

John 1:51: "Then he said, 'I tell you the truth, you will all see heaven open and the angels of God going up and down on the Son of Man, the one who is the stairway between heaven and earth.'" NIV

1 Timothy 2:5: "For, there is one God and one Mediator who can reconcile God and humanity—the man Christ Jesus." NIV

Romans 5:8: "But God showed his great love for us by sending Christ to die for us while we were still sinners." NIV

6

The FRUIT
of LOVE

1 **Corinthians 8:1 says that knowledge puffs up, while love builds up.** If you've ever seen what heat does to a marshmallow, or how heat and spinning turns sugar into cotton candy, you might be able to picture this.

Another example is how a kitten looks when it feels threatened. But when things are puffed up, they haven't actually become any larger or more powerful; the increase is just an illusion.

Sometimes when people begin to study and learn, they grow proud—they feel larger and more important. The more they learn and understand, the bigger they become—in their own eyes. The more important they feel, the less respect and love they show toward others.

Beware of this trap! If we grow proud, we will become God's enemies and He will stop revealing Himself to us. Let's read some verses that show this truth:

PROVERBS 3:7:

"Do not be wise in your own eyes; fear the LORD and shun evil."

JAMES 4:6-10:

". . . he gives grace generously. As the Scriptures say, 'God opposes the proud but gives grace to the humble.' 7 So humble yourselves before God. Resist the devil, and he will flee from you. 8 Come close to God, and God will come close to you. Wash your hands, you sinners; purify your hearts, for your loyalty is divided between God and the world. 9 Let there be tears for what you have done. Let there be sorrow and deep grief. Let there be sadness instead of laughter, and gloom instead of joy.

10 Humble yourselves before the Lord, and he will lift you up in honor."

Don't be wise in your own eyes.

29. According to James 4:6, *who* does God oppose, resist or fight against?

30. James 4:7 tells us to do *something* before (and while) resisting the devil. What is it?

HE GIVES GRACE to the HUMBLE

God is against the proud but He gives grace to the humble. The Bible is *His Word* to you, therefore, you don't have to be intelligent or educated to understand the Scriptures—but you must be humble!

If you come to God humbly, asking Jesus to show Himself to you, and to explain His words to you, He will. If you believe and are born again, Scripture says you "have the mind of Christ" inside of you.

READ 1 CORINTHIANS 2:16:

... "'Who can know the Lord's thoughts? Who knows enough to teach him?' But we understand these things, for we have the mind of Christ."

NOW READ 1 CORINTHIANS 1:26-29:

"Remember, dear brothers and sisters, that few of you were wise in the world's eyes or powerful or wealthy when God called you. 27 Instead, God chose things the world considers foolish in order to shame those who think they are wise. And he chose things that are powerless to shame those who are powerful. 28 God chose things despised by the world, things counted as nothing at all, and used them to bring to nothing what the world considers important. 29 As a result, no one can ever boast in the presence of God."

God chooses the foolish things of the world to shame those who are wise in their own eyes. If you ever feel tempted to boast that you have knowledge of God and His Word, don't do it! The moment you begin to boast, you turn against the One who has been revealing Himself to you.

NEW LIFE; NEW SPIRIT

There is only one God, and He consists of three persons: God the Father, Jesus the Son, and the Holy Spirit. John Chapter One tells us that Jesus is the Creator of all things, who came to earth.

Jesus created you and He wants you to know Him as He knows you.

READ 1 JOHN 4:9-10:

"God showed how much he loved us by sending his one and only Son into the world so that we might have eternal life through him. 10 This is real love— not that we loved God, but that he loved us and sent his Son as a sacrifice to take away our sins."

God is love. We've learned that God showed us His love through the cross. But look at the next verse:

READ VERSE 11:

"Dear friends, since God loved us that much, we surely ought to love each other."

God loves us so much that He went to the cross for us. But now we are expected to respond. How are we supposed to respond? By loving each other.

When Jesus came to earth and died on the cross for your sins, He showed you the love God has for you. But He also showed you the love He has for everyone around you. He loves them!

When we find Jesus, if we truly believe and trust Him, we will react by loving Him and loving each other. There will be a change inside of us, and that inside change will show on the outside too.

LET'S READ VERSES 12-13:

"No one has ever seen God. But if we love each other, God lives in us, and his love is brought to full expression in us. 13 And God has given us his Spirit as proof that we live in him and he in us."

When we believe, we ask Jesus to forgive us — He then sends His Holy Spirit to live inside of us. This is why we react by loving others.

When God's loving Holy Spirit moves inside of us, He begins to love people through our lives.

If you do not see God's love working inside of you, maybe you do not have His Spirit inside of you. As we've read earlier, anyone who does not have the Spirit of Christ does not belong to Him. If you don't have the Holy Spirit, you have no proof that you're *in Christ*. So ask Him to fill you with His Holy Spirit and to change you.

LIVING PROOF

We are studying the book of John. We've been studying verse by verse and we're in John Chapter One.

LET'S READ VERSE 19-27:

"This was John's testimony when the Jewish leaders sent priests and Temple assistants from Jerusalem to ask John, 'Who are you?' 20 He came right out and said, 'I am not the Messiah.'

21 'Well then, who are you?' they asked. 'Are you Elijah?'

'No,' he replied.

'Are you the Prophet we are expecting?'

'No.'

22 'Then who are you? We need an answer for those who sent us. What do you have to say about yourself?'

23 John replied in the words of the prophet Isaiah: 'I am a voice shouting in the wilderness, "Clear the way for the Lord's coming!"'

24 Then the Pharisees who had been sent **25** asked him, 'If you aren't the Messiah or Elijah or the Prophet, what right do you have to baptize?'

26 John told them, 'I baptize with water, but right here in the crowd is someone you do not recognize. **27** Though his ministry follows mine, I'm not even worthy to be his slave and untie the straps of his sandal.'"

John the Baptist prepared people for Jesus to come. After that, Jesus began His ministry. Turn to Matthew Chapter Three, and we'll read about this same time, from another eye-witness's point of view.

READ MATTHEW 3:7-8:

"But when he saw many Pharisees and Sadducees coming to be baptized, he [John] denounced them. 'You brood of snakes!' he exclaimed. 'Who warned you to flee the coming wrath? **8** Prove by the way you live that you have repented of your sins and turned to God.'"

John the Baptist knew that the anger of God was coming because of sins. When religious people came to be baptized, he told them to prove that they had repented.

Repent means to turn away, and to turn around and go the opposite direction. How can we prove that we are repenting from our sins and turning to God? Read verse 8 again. We prove we have repented *by the way we live.* When we repent, we stop sinning against God and against people. We start loving God and loving people. To repent means to change how you live.

READ VERSES 9-10:

"Don't just say to each other, 'We're safe, for we are descendants of Abraham.' That means nothing, for I tell you, God can create children of Abraham from these very stones. 10 Even now the ax of God's judgment is poised, ready to sever the roots of the trees. Yes, every tree that does not produce good fruit will be chopped down and thrown into the fire."

When you see the fruit of God's Spirit in your life, this is proof that you have His Spirit. The good fruit you will produce is love—God's love. Keep your finger in Matthew Chapter Three.

LET'S READ GALATIANS 5:22-25:

"But the Holy Spirit produces this kind of fruit in our lives: love, joy, peace, patience, kindness, goodness, faithfulness, 23 gentleness, and self-control. There is no law against these things! 24 Those who belong to Christ Jesus have nailed the passions and desires of their sinful nature to his cross and crucified them there. 25 Since we are living by the Spirit, let us follow the Spirit's leading in every part of our lives."

These verses tell us what God's love *looks like*. When we come to Christ, we must turn away from our sins and allow God to work inside of us. The Spirit will lead us to do loving things. He will grow the fruit of His love in us.

We will love other people for His glory and by His power.

Let's return to Matthew Chapter Three, where John is still talking about Jesus.

READ MATTHEW 3:11-12:

> "I baptize with water those who repent of their sins and turn to God. But someone is coming soon who is greater than I am—so much greater that I'm not worthy even to be his slave and carry his sandals. He will baptize you with the Holy Spirit and with fire. 12 He is ready to separate the chaff from the wheat with his winnowing fork. Then he will clean up the threshing area, gathering the wheat into his barn but burning the chaff with never-ending fire."

John baptized with water, but Jesus was coming. Jesus baptizes us with his Holy Spirit and fire.

Baptism is a symbol of death. Going under the water symbolizes dying to your old life, dying to your sinful nature, dying to self, and being raised up to live a new life. John the Baptist told people to prove they had repented of their sins; prove it by living changed lives. Now Jesus has come. We repent and are baptized into his death, and we are raised to new life. And then something more happens—we are filled with His Holy Spirit. We are baptized in God's Spirit and fire. But go back and read verse 12 again:

> **"He is ready to separate the chaff from the wheat with his winnowing fork. Then he will clean up the threshing area, gathering the wheat into his barn but burning the chaff with never-ending fire."**

Who will separate the chaff from the wheat? Jesus. Who will gather the wheat into his barn? Jesus. But the chaff will be burned with never-ending fire. This is not speaking of literal wheat and chaff. Do you remember what John said to the religious people in verse 8?

> **"Prove by the way you live that you have repented of your sins and turned to God."**

> **NOW READ JOHN 15:8:**

> **Jesus said, "This is to my Father's glory, that you bear much fruit, showing yourselves to be my disciples." NIV**

Coming to Jesus requires belief. True belief causes us to repent of our sins and live changed lives, filled with God's Holy Spirit. *He* will love people through our lives.

Our old sinful nature will still exist, but the power of God's Spirit will enable us to deny and break free from our fallen nature. He will lead us to hate sin, to love people, and to love God. This is God's plan and what His Spirit wants to do in us.

The Holy Spirit's fruit is the proof that we actually belong to Jesus and have His Spirit inside of us.

READ 2 CORINTHIANS 7:1:

"Because we have these promises, dear friends, let us cleanse ourselves from everything that can defile our body or spirit. And let us work toward complete holiness because we fear God."

31. Do you have any enemies that hate you, or that you dislike?

32. Do they know that Jesus loves them and died on the cross to take away their sin?

If you put your faith in Christ, the Bible says you are born again—born of the Spirit of God. Scripture says you have the Holy Spirit inside of you, and you have the mind of Christ.

You don't have to be highly educated to know Jesus or understand His Word. You just need *the Spirit of the Word* inside of you.

Come to Him humbly and ask Him to show Himself to you. Ask Him to explain His words to you. But when He does, you must respond!

HOMEWORK:

If you don't see God's love working inside of you—if you are not growing His fruit in your life—ask Him to fill you with His Holy Spirit and to change you.

If you've finished reading the Gospels of Matthew, Mark, Luke and John, and the book of Acts, begin reading the rest of the New Testament—one book at a time. Start with the book of Romans. Always pray before you read. Ask the Spirit of Jesus to open your understanding and explain His Word.

PRACTICE THESE MEMORY VERSES:

1 Corinthians 1:27: "But God chose the foolish things of the world to shame the wise; God chose the weak things of the world to shame the strong."

Galatians 5:22-23: "But the fruit of the Spirit is love, joy, peace, forbearance, kindness, goodness, faithfulness, 23 gentleness and self-control. Against such things there is no law."

1 John 4:10-11: "This is love: not that we loved God, but that he loved us and sent his Son as an atoning sacrifice for our sins. 11 Dear friends, since God so loved us, we also ought to love one another."

7

The LAMB of GOD

We have been studying the Bible to find Jesus. This week we'll see that Jesus is the *Lamb of God* who takes away the sin of the world. And hopefully we'll begin to understand what that means in our lives.

Let's continue reading about John the Baptist from John Chapter One where we left off last time.

READ JOHN 1:29-36:

"The next day John saw Jesus coming toward him and said, 'Look! The Lamb of God who takes away the sin of the world! 30 He is the one I was talking about when I said, "A man is coming after me who is far greater than I am, for he existed long before me." 31 I did not recognize him as the Messiah, but I have been baptizing with water so that he might be revealed to Israel.'

32 Then John testified, 'I saw the Holy Spirit descending like a dove from heaven and resting upon him. 33 I didn't know he was the one, but when God sent me to baptize with water, he told me, "The one on whom you see the Spirit descend and rest is the one who will baptize with the Holy Spirit." 34 I saw this happen to Jesus, so I testify that he is the Chosen One of God.' 35 The following day John was again standing with two of his disciples. 36 As Jesus walked by, John looked at him and declared, 'Look! There is the Lamb of God!'"

John called Jesus "the Lamb of God who takes away the sin of the world." What does that mean?

Remember: the only accurate and safe way to study the Bible is to let the Bible interpret itself. So to understand what John meant, we search the Bible for this subject—beginning with the *first mention.*

The first lambs specifically mentioned in the Bible belonged to Adam and Eve's son Abel. He raised sheep and brought the firstlings to God—and *his offering pleased God.* But the first time a sacrifice was made to cover sin was earlier, when Adam and Eve sinned in the garden. God killed an animal and made clothing from animal skins to cover their shame. I suspect it was a lamb, because of everything that followed.

However, we know for sure that Adam and Eve died spiritually when they rebelled against God's command. After that, every person was born spiritually dead and with a sinful nature. When God covered Adam and Eve's shame through an animal sacrifice, He foretold the future. He had a plan to revive mankind. It involved a lamb suffering to pay for their sin.

> 33. Where can you find the "first mention" of a lamb in the Bible?
>
> 34. Where is the first sacrifice in the Bible?

THE SUBSTITUTE LAMB

The truth that sin *forfeits the life of the guilty one* is established all throughout the Scriptures. But so is the fact that the blood of an innocent *substitutionary* sacrifice could cover sin and remove guilt.

READ LEVITICUS 17:11:

> "... for the life of the body is in its blood. I have given you the blood on the altar to purify you, making you right with the Lord. It is the blood, given in exchange for a life, that makes purification possible."

Innocent blood (given in exchange for a life that was forfeited due to sin), made purification and release from guilt possible.

READ ALSO HEBREWS 9:22:

". . . according to the law of Moses, nearly everything was purified with blood. For without the shedding of blood, there is no forgiveness."

Throughout history God continued to show that His plan always involved an innocent lamb dying as a sacrifice or covering for man's sin. For example:

READ GENESIS 22:8:

"'God will provide a lamb for the burnt offering, my son,' Abraham answered. And they both walked on together."

In this story, God tested Abraham's faith by commanding: "Take your son, your only son—yes, Isaac, whom you love so much—and go to the land of Moriah. Go and sacrifice him as a burnt offering on one of the mountains, which I will show you." Though heartbroken, Abraham was willing to obey, knowing God could also raise his son from the dead.

To Abraham it was obvious that his son would ultimately *live*—God had promised his son would grow to manhood and be a father. So Abraham revealed his complete trust in God's promises. But on the mountain God told him not to harm his son, and instead God provided a sacrifice—a ram caught by its horns in the brush. Abraham sacrificed the sheep, instead of his son.

What does this have to do with Jesus? Abraham and his "only son" were told by God to perform this sacrifice on the same exact mountain that God's only son Jesus would later be crucified on—*during Passover.*

THE LAMB WHO SAVES

Passover originated when God brought His people out of slavery in Egypt, about 1500 years before Jesus died on the cross. Once again God showed that His plan to save mankind would involve a lamb suffering and dying for the people.

During their time of deliverance, God instructed His people to sacrifice a lamb and put its blood across the posts of their door. During the Passover, the angel of death passed over the homes that were protected by the blood of the lamb.

Here's another prophecy about the Lamb who would come to save the world:

READ ISAIAH 53:7:

"He was oppressed, and he was afflicted, yet he opened not his mouth; like a lamb that is led to the slaughter, and like a sheep that before its shearers is silent, so he opened not his mouth."

We see in Romans 3:23, and other places in Scripture, that all people are guilty. All people have sinned and they fall short of God's glory; they are not living up to what God created them for—to be in His righteous image, and to live in intimate fellowship with Him.

Sin separates us from God. Sin forfeits our life and stains us. Yet, since the beginning, God has made a way to restore us to fellowship with Him—but that can only be done when we are clean. God is holy, and nothing sinful can enter His presence.

Let's read from Hebrews Chapter Ten. This is a prophecy that spoke of Jesus, long before He came.

READ HEBREWS 10:1-2:

"The old system under the law of Moses was only a shadow, a dim preview of the good things to come, not the good things themselves. The sacrifices under that system were repeated again and again, year after year, but they were never able to provide perfect cleansing for those who came to worship. 2 If they could have provided perfect cleansing, the sacrifices would have stopped, for the worshipers would have been purified once for all time, and their feelings of guilt would have disappeared."

The sacrifices of animals only *covered* sin—they did not permanently cleanse. They did not remove

the feelings of guilt, but served as a constant reminder of sin.

NOW READ VERSES 3-7:

"But instead, those sacrifices actually reminded them of their sins year after year. 4 For it is not possible for the blood of bulls and goats to take away sins. 5 That is why, when Christ came into the world, he said to God, 'You did not want animal sacrifices or sin offerings. But you have given me a body to offer. 6 You were not pleased with burnt offerings or other offerings for sin. 7 Then I said, "Look, I have come to do your will, O God — as is written about me in the Scriptures."'"

Jesus was a *better sacrifice.* It was not possible for the blood of animals to take away sins, but the sacrifice of Christ's body made permanent forgiveness possible.

READ VERSES 8-10:

"First, Christ said, 'You did not want animal sacrifices or sin offerings or burnt offerings or other offerings for sin, nor were you pleased with them' (though they are required by the law of Moses). 9 Then he said, 'Look, I have come to do your will.' He cancels the first covenant in order to put the second into effect. 10 For God's will was for us to be made holy by the sacrifice of the body of Jesus Christ, once for all time."

When Jesus came, the sacrifice of animals was ended. Jesus was the perfect Lamb of God, the sinless perfect sacrifice. His blood did not just cover sin. His blood permanently washed away the sins of those who put their trust in Him.

> **In Matthew 26:28 Jesus said: ". . . for this is my blood, which confirms the covenant between God and his people. It is poured out as a sacrifice to forgive the sins of many."**

Here are some more verses on this subject:

> **Isaiah 1:18: "'Come now, let's settle this,' says the LORD. 'Though your sins are like scarlet, I will make them as white as snow. Though they are red like crimson, I will make them as white as wool.'"**

> **John 3:14-16: "And as Moses lifted up the bronze snake on a pole in the wilderness, so the Son of Man must be lifted up, 15 so that everyone who believes in him will have eternal life. 16 'For this is how God loved the world: He gave his one and only Son, so that everyone who believes in him will not perish but have eternal life.'"**

> **Revelation 5:12-13: "And they sang in a mighty chorus: 'Worthy is the Lamb who was slaughtered — to receive power and riches and wisdom and strength and honor and glory and blessing.' 13 And then I heard every creature in heaven and on earth and under the earth and in the sea. They sang: 'Blessing and honor**

and glory and power belong to the one sitting on the throne and to the Lamb forever and ever.'"

35. According to John 3:14-16, why was it necessary for Jesus to be lifted up on a cross?

36. According to Matthew 26:28, why was Jesus' blood "poured out"?

THE LAMB HAS a BOOK

Jesus is the Lamb of God who takes away the sin of the world—but only for those who believe and receive Him. Read these verses:

Revelation 13:8: "And all the people who belong to this world worshiped the beast. They are the ones whose names were not written in the Book of Life that belongs to the Lamb who was slaughtered before the world was made."

Revelation 20:15: "And anyone whose name was not found recorded in the Book of Life was thrown into the lake of fire."

Revelation 21:27: "Nothing evil will be allowed to enter, nor anyone who practices shameful idolatry and dishonesty—but only those whose names are written in the Lamb's Book of Life."

These verses also talk about the Lamb's Book of Life:

Exodus 32:31-33, Psalms 69:28, Daniel 12:1, Malachi 3:16, Luke 10:20, Philippians 4:3, Revelation 3:1-6, Revelation 17:8, and Revelation 20:11-15.

Have you put your trust in Jesus? Is your name written in His book? He is the Lamb of God who is willing to take your sin away, forever.

HOMEWORK:

Continue studying the books of the New Testament as explained last week. Ask Jesus to help you to stay in step with His Holy Spirit; He will lead you into all truth.

PRACTICE THESE MEMORY VERSES:

Hebrews 9:22: ". . . according to the law of Moses, nearly everything was purified with blood. For without the shedding of blood, there is no forgiveness." NIV

Isaiah 1:18: "'Come now, let's settle this,' says the LORD. 'Though your sins are like scarlet, I will make them as white as snow. Though they are red like crimson, I will make them as white as wool.'" NIV

Revelation 20:15: "And anyone whose name was not found recorded in the Book of Life was thrown into the lake of fire." NIV

8

FOLLOWING the LAMB

Jesus is the Messiah; He is the **Savior promised by God through His prophets.** When Jesus came to earth, people were waiting for the Savior. But most people did not accept Him. They rejected Him because He was not the type of Savior they wanted.

Let's look at one of the prophecies that told of the coming Messiah. This was written long before Jesus was born, but it spoke of Him:

"For a child is born to us, a son is given to us. The government will rest on his shoulders. And he will be called: Wonderful Counselor, Mighty God, Everlasting Father, Prince of Peace. 7 His government and its peace will never end. He will rule with fairness and justice from the throne of his ancestor David for all eternity. The passionate commitment of the Lord of Heaven's Armies will make this happen!"

This prophecy promised that a child would be born—He would be unlike any other child who ever lived. He would be *Mighty God* and *Everlasting Father.* He would live forever—His kingdom would be eternal. This would be hard to imagine, but the nation, as a whole, believed that this divine Messiah would come. But now take a look at the verses just before that prophecy:

Read verses 2-5:

"The people who walk in darkness will see a great light. For those who live in a land of deep darkness, a light will shine. 3 You will enlarge the nation of Israel, and its people will rejoice. They will rejoice before you as people rejoice at the harvest and like warriors dividing the plunder. 4 For you will break the yoke of their slavery and lift the heavy burden from their shoulders. You will break the oppressor's rod, just as you did when you destroyed the army of Midian. 5 The boots of the warrior and the uniforms bloodstained by war will all be burned. They will be fuel for the fire."

This prophecy could easily be promising a political and national leader. So it isn't surprising that the people were looking for a Savior who would liberate their nation, in a political sense.

When Jesus came, enemy forces occupied the nation, and this section of the prophecy seems to promise political victory; it speaks of the nation being enlarged and victorious warriors. They were more than ready to welcome their long-awaited Messiah. And they had many plans for Him when He came!

> 37. If you made a list of your biggest problems and needs, what would your top three be?
>
> 38. Have you taken your list to Jesus and asked Him to fix these problems? What was the result?

CHASING the LAMB

We have been studying the book of John. Open your Bibles to John Chapter One.

LET'S READ JOHN 1:35-37:

"The following day John was again standing with two of his disciples. 36 As Jesus walked by, John looked at him and declared, 'Look! There is the Lamb of God!' 37 When John's two disciples heard this, they followed Jesus."

John the Baptist pointed out Jesus and called Him the Lamb of God. Upon hearing this, two of his disciples immediately followed Jesus. Many people believe that Jesus is the Savior. But how many people will drop everything to chase after Him?

Would you leave everything behind, to have only Jesus? That is what these men did.

WHAT DO YOU WANT?

READ VERSES 38-42:

"Jesus looked around and saw them following. 'What do you want?' he asked them.

They replied, 'Rabbi' (which means "Teacher"), 'where are you staying?'

39 'Come and see,' he said. It was about four o'clock in the afternoon when they went with him to the place where he was staying, and they remained with him the rest of the day.

40 Andrew, Simon Peter's brother, was one of these men who heard what John said and then followed Jesus. 41 Andrew went to find his brother, Simon, and told him, 'We have found the Messiah' (which means "Christ").

42 Then Andrew brought Simon to meet Jesus. Looking intently at Simon, Jesus said, 'Your name is Si-

mon, son of John—but you will be called Cephas' (which means "Peter")."

Jesus asked these men, "What do you want?" They could have asked Him for anything—He is God; He literally could have given them anything or everything they could imagine. Most people who come to Jesus want something from Him. And that's not a bad thing; the Bible tells us to ask God for what we need. He wants us to come to Him with our needs and to completely depend upon Him. However, these men didn't ask Him for anything. They just wanted to know where He was staying. They wanted to spend time with Him.

They didn't ask Him for healing. They didn't ask Him to solve their problems. They didn't ask Him to bless them or help them pay their bills. They didn't ask for daily bread. They didn't even ask Him how they could get to heaven.

They wanted to be as close to Jesus as they could. They wanted to stay where He stays and to follow Him around. And they wanted to bring other people close to Him too. Do you think, maybe, this is why Jesus chose these men?

LET'S READ VERSES 43-47:

"The next day Jesus decided to go to Galilee. He found Philip and said to him, 'Come, follow me.' 44 Philip was from Bethsaida, Andrew and Peter's hometown. 45 Philip went to look for Nathanael and told him, 'We have found the very person Moses and the prophets wrote about! His name is Jesus, the son of Joseph from Nazareth.'

46 'Nazareth!' exclaimed Nathanael. 'Can anything good come from Nazareth?'

'Come and see for yourself,' Philip replied.

47 As they approached, Jesus said, 'Now here is a genuine son of Israel — a man of complete integrity.'"

These men had been looking for the Messiah, the Savior — but so were the other people in their country. The religious leaders taught the Scriptures, so they knew a Savior would come. But most of them were not looking for a *spiritual* Messiah. They wanted a political Savior — a king who would set them free from the control of the Roman government. The leaders didn't want a Messiah who would come and tell them to repent and stop sinning.

They weren't interested in holiness; they wanted liberty and prosperity.

However, these uneducated fishermen and other unimportant men were also waiting and looking for the Savior. And when Jesus came, they received Him. They accepted Him and allowed the Messiah to be whoever and whatever He was.

Will we receive Jesus just as He is and seek Him because we want to know Him? Or are we just looking for a really powerful servant?

WHERE ARE YOU STAYING?

READ JOHN 6:48-53:

"Jesus said, 'Yes, I am the bread of life! 49 Your ancestors ate manna in the wilderness, but they all died. 50 Anyone who eats the bread from heaven, however, will never die. 51 I am the living bread that came down from heaven. Anyone who eats this bread will live forever; and this bread, which I will offer so the world may live, is my flesh.'

52 Then the people began arguing with each other about what he meant. 'How can this man give us his flesh to eat?" they asked.'

53 So Jesus said again, 'I tell you the truth, unless you eat the flesh of the Son of Man and drink his blood, you cannot have eternal life within you.'"

Jesus was very popular for awhile. Great crowds followed Him. But they were only looking for a better life *now*. Of course they wanted to go to heaven some day. But the afterlife wasn't the focus of their lives.

Most people were searching for a practical Savior, one who could give them peace, safety, and prosperity in this life.

When Jesus didn't meet their expectations (and He started talking about difficult spiritual matters), they stopped following Him.

"At this point many of his disciples turned away and deserted him. 67 Then Jesus turned to the Twelve and asked, 'Are you also going to leave?'

68 Simon Peter replied, 'Lord, to whom would we go? You have the words that give eternal life. 69 We believe, and we know you are the Holy One of God.'"

Jesus asked the twelve disciples if they were also going to leave Him. Peter answered for them; they knew that Jesus was the Holy One of God—they knew that His words would give them eternal life. Despite His hard sayings, they were staying.

Likewise, we must believe He is the *Holy One of God* and that He is the only one whose words lead to eternal life. We must be ready to accept Him as He is, and to drop everything so we can follow Him around and serve Him.

39. In John 6:68, what did Peter say about the words of Jesus?

40. Have you found any hard or offensive sayings in the Bible? How did you respond?

GREATER THINGS

READ JOHN 1:48-51:

"'How do you know about me?' Nathanael asked.

Jesus replied, 'I could see you under the fig tree before Philip found you.'

49 Then Nathanael exclaimed, 'Rabbi, you are the Son of God—the King of Israel!'

50 Jesus asked him, 'Do you believe this just because I told you I had seen you under the fig tree? You will see greater things than this.' 51 Then he said, 'I tell you the truth, you will all see heaven open and the angels of God going up and down on the Son of Man, the one who is the stairway between heaven and earth.'"

Jesus is the King—the eternal King. And Jesus told these men they would see greater things, because they dropped everything to follow Him.

Did all people see these greater things? No. Many people rejected Jesus. He wasn't what they wanted and they didn't want to lose anything to be close to Him.

Most of the crowd gave up *greater things* in order to hold on to what they already had. It's the same today.

Most people will not see heaven open. They will not see the angels of God going up and down on the Son of Man. They might pray to Jesus and ask Him for help now and then. But they don't really want to know Him. They won't give up their own lives to follow Him around and serve Him. They want something *from Jesus,* but they do not want Jesus Himself. So they will not see great things.

Most people will not find the stairway between heaven and earth, because they won't risk anything looking for it.

ONLY JESUS = EVERYTHING YOU NEED

LET'S READ MATTHEW 19:16-22:

"Someone came to Jesus with this question: 'Teacher, what good deed must I do to have eternal life?'

17 'Why ask me about what is good?' Jesus replied. 'There is only One who is good. But to answer your question—if you want to receive eternal life, keep the commandments.'

18 'Which ones?' the man asked.

And Jesus replied: 'You must not murder. You must not commit adultery. You must not steal. You must not testify falsely. 19 Honor your father and mother. Love your neighbor as yourself.'

20 'I've obeyed all these commandments,' the young man replied. 'What else must I do?'

21 Jesus told him, 'If you want to be perfect, go and sell all your possessions and give the money to the

98

poor, and you will have treasure in heaven. Then come, follow me.'

22 But when the young man heard this, he went away sad, for he had many possessions."

This young man went away sad. He wasn't willing to give up his own life and his many possessions. He wasn't satisfied to have *only Jesus.*

READ VERSES 23-30:

23 "Then Jesus said to his disciples, 'I tell you the truth, it is very hard for a rich person to enter the Kingdom of Heaven. 24 I'll say it again—it is easier for a camel to go through the eye of a needle than for a rich person to enter the Kingdom of God!'

25 The disciples were astounded. 'Then who in the world can be saved?' they asked.

26 Jesus looked at them intently and said, 'Humanly speaking, it is impossible. But with God everything is possible.'

27 Then Peter said to him, 'We've given up everything to follow you. What will we get?'

28 Jesus replied, 'I assure you that when the world is made new and the Son of Man sits upon his glorious throne, you who have been my followers will also sit on twelve thrones, judging the twelve tribes of Israel. 29 And everyone who has given up houses or brothers or sisters or father or mother or children or property,

for my sake, will receive a hundred times as much in return and will inherit eternal life. 30 But many who are the greatest now will be least important then, and those who seem least important now will be the greatest then.'"

These men left everything just to follow Jesus. They just wanted to know Jesus; they wanted to know where He was staying and to be close to Him. But Jesus says they will receive many blessings in return. I hope and pray that we will be like these men!

It isn't wrong for us to bring our troubles to Jesus. It's good to ask Him to meet our needs. In fact:

READ PHILIPPIANS 4:6-7:

"Don't worry about anything; instead, pray about everything. Tell God what you need, and thank him for all he has done. Then you will experience God's peace, which exceeds anything we can understand. His peace will guard your hearts and minds as you live in Christ Jesus."

Tell God what you need, and thank Him. Then let it go; don't give it anymore thought. Spend your energy seeking Jesus and righteousness. If you seek Jesus and His kingdom, you will have everything you need.

READ MATTHEW 6:31-33:

Jesus said, "'So don't worry about these things, saying, "What will we eat? What will we drink? What will we wear?" 32 These things dominate the thoughts of unbelievers, but your heavenly Father already knows all your needs. 33 Seek the Kingdom of God above all else, and live righteously, and he will give you everything you need.'"

HOMEWORK:

Continue reading through the books of the New Testament as explained last week. Ask Jesus to help you and to explain what you're reading. Ask Him to help you to stay in step with the Holy Spirit and to lead you into all truth.

PRACTICE THESE MEMORY VERSES:

Isaiah 9:6: "For to us a child is born, to us a son is given, and the government will be on his shoulders. And he will be called Wonderful Counselor, Mighty God, Everlasting Father, Prince of Peace." NIV

John 6:67-68: "'You do not want to leave too, do you?' Jesus asked the Twelve. 68 Simon Peter answered him, 'Lord, to whom shall we go? You have the words of eternal life.'" NIV

Matthew 6:33: "But seek first his kingdom and his righteousness, and all these things will be given to you as well." NIV

9

INVITED to a WEDDING

The Bible declares many times **that there is only one God.** And we see through the Scriptures that the Creator of all things is one God in three persons: God the Father, Jesus the Son, and the Holy Spirit.

We've learned that Jesus is God in the flesh. He is the Creator of all things. Jesus reveals the Father God to us, so we've been studying the Bible to find Jesus. We've also learned that Jesus is called the *Lamb of God*. He was the final, perfect sacrifice.

His death upon the cross provides cleansing and forgiveness for all who will receive Him. But there's more about the Lamb of God in Scripture. And remember, as you study, ask Jesus to open your understanding. Don't look to outside writings or the opinions of men.

Let the Spirit of Christ and the Bible explain the Bible to you. To understand one scripture, read many other scriptures.

With that in mind, let's read from Revelation to learn more about the Lamb:

READ REVELATION 19:9A:

"And the angel said to me, 'Write this: Blessed are those who are invited to the wedding feast of the Lamb.'"

The Lamb is getting married?! Yes. The Father has planned a wedding for His Son at the end of the age. Jesus is often referred to as the bridegroom, and the church is His chosen bride. And the time we currently live in can be clearly seen in this parable that Jesus told:

READ MATTHEW 22:2-6:

"The Kingdom of Heaven can be illustrated by the story of a king who prepared a great wedding feast for his son. 3 When the banquet was ready, he sent his

servants to notify those who were invited. But they all refused to come!

4 So he sent other servants to tell them, 'The feast has been prepared. The bulls and fattened cattle have been killed, and everything is ready. Come to the banquet!' 5 But the guests he had invited ignored them and went their own way, one to his farm, another to his business. 6 Others seized his messengers and insulted them and killed them."

In this parable the wedding feast has been prepared and the servants have been sent out to invite the guests—but the guests are unwilling to come.

We're living in this time.

COME to the WEDDING!

We (believers) are the servants. But inviting people to the wedding of the Lamb can be a dangerous job. In fact, more than 70 million Christians have been martyred in the course of history. More than half were martyred in the 20th century under communist and fascist governments.

Between 2000 and 2010, roughly 1,093,000 Christians were martyred worldwide. Remember, if these servants hid their faith and refused to deliver the message, they wouldn't have suffered persecution. These sad statistics prove that the King's servants have been faithfully inviting people to the feast.

"The king was furious, and he sent out his army to destroy the murderers and burn their town. 8 And he said to his servants, 'The wedding feast is ready, and the guests I invited aren't worthy of the honor. 9 Now go out to the street corners and invite everyone you see.' 10 So the servants brought in everyone they could find, good and bad alike, and the banquet hall was filled with guests.

11 But when the king came in to meet the guests, he noticed a man who wasn't wearing the proper clothes for a wedding. 12 'Friend,' he asked, 'how is it that you are here without wedding clothes?' But the man had no reply. 13 Then the king said to his aides, 'Bind his hands and feet and throw him into the outer darkness, where there will be weeping and gnashing of teeth. 14 For many are called, but few are chosen.'"

The people who were invited first rejected the invitation, and that opened the way for many others to be invited. But notice what happened when a man tried to attend this wedding without the proper wedding clothes. He was cast out.

GET YOUR WEDDING CLOTHES ON!

The Bible tell us that Christ dresses His people in white garments, also called "fine linen, white and clean." Fine linen stands for righteous behavior. These white garments were washed clean in the blood of the Lamb and they're expected to keep them spotless.

"They have washed their robes in the blood of the Lamb and made them white."

This doesn't only speak of going to Jesus and asking for forgiveness, but also of living in intimate union with Christ—which changes us on the inside and the outside.

READ REVELATION 19:8:

"'She has been given the finest of pure white linen to wear.' For the fine linen represents the good deeds of God's holy people."

ROMANS 13:13-14 SAYS IT LIKE THIS:

"Because we belong to the day, we must live decent lives for all to see. Don't participate in the darkness of wild parties and drunkenness, or in sexual promiscuity and immoral living, or in quarreling and jealousy. 14 Instead, clothe yourself with the presence of the Lord Jesus Christ. And don't let yourself think about ways to indulge your evil desires."

What does it mean to clothe yourself with the presence of Jesus? Live decent lives. Walk in the light. Don't get drunk, and don't be sexually immoral. Don't fight; don't be jealous.

Don't even let yourself think about doing evil things. This is what it means to live in union with Christ, clothed with Jesus.

Jesus said, "Remain in me, and I will remain in you. For a branch cannot produce fruit if it is severed from the vine, and you cannot be fruitful unless you remain in me.

Yes, I am the vine; you are the branches. Those who remain in me, and I in them, will produce much fruit. For apart from me you can do nothing."

Clothe yourself with Christ; remain in Him and He will remain in you. This will keep your garments spotless and prepare you for the marriage supper of the Lamb.

41. At the "Wedding Feast of the Lamb," who will the bride and bridegroom be?

42. According to Rev. 13, what were the robes washed in to make them white and spotless?

GOING to the CHAPEL

We're still studying the book of John; we're in Chapter Two.

READ JOHN 2:1-2:

"The next day there was a wedding celebration in the village of Cana in Galilee. Jesus' mother was there, 2 and Jesus and his disciples were also invited to the celebration."

Jesus performed His first public miracle at a wedding. That's very significant. Also, He did this miracle because someone believed in His power and asked Him for help—which is also significant. His character is perfectly consistent throughout Scripture. We learn to know Jesus better from these facts.

READ VERSES 3-11:

"The wine supply ran out during the festivities, so Jesus' mother told him, 'They have no more wine.'

4'Dear woman, that's not our problem,' Jesus replied. 'My time has not yet come.'

5 But his mother told the servants, 'Do whatever he tells you.'

6 Standing nearby were six stone water jars, used for Jewish ceremonial washing. Each could hold twenty to thirty gallons. 7 Jesus told the servants, 'Fill the jars with water.' When the jars had been filled, 8 he said, 'Now dip some out, and take it to the master of ceremonies.' So the servants followed his instructions. 9 When the master of ceremonies tasted the water that was now wine, not knowing where it had come from (though, of course, the servants knew), he called the bridegroom over.

10 'A host always serves the best wine first,' he said. 'Then, when everyone has had a lot to drink, he brings out the less expensive wine. But you have kept the best until now!'

11 This miraculous sign at Cana in Galilee was the first time Jesus revealed his glory. And his disciples believed in him."

Some people are confused by this miracle, either because they haven't studied the whole Bible on this subject, or because they've been misled by a false teacher. Jesus is not telling us to drink wine; He's not saying it is okay to become drunk. But marriage is a very important theme in the Bible.

This miracle was not intended to make us think about wine. Jesus wanted us to notice that He began His ministry at a wedding.

MISSING the WEDDING

Many people will miss the main point, the wedding, because they're distracted by wine. Alcoholic drinks have always had a powerful ability to seduce people and dull their senses; if they give in to its pull, they'll miss everything they should have noticed and lose everything they should have held on to. Many scriptures warn about the dangers of drinking alcohol and wine. Consider these verses:

Proverbs 20:1: "Wine produces mockers; alcohol leads to brawls. Those led astray by drink cannot be wise."

Luke 21:34: "Watch out! Don't let your hearts be dulled by carousing and drunkenness, and by the

worries of this life. Don't let that day catch you un-
aware . . ."

Romans 13:13a: "Because we belong to the day, we
must live decent lives for all to see. Don't participate
in the darkness of wild parties and drunkenness . . ."

What could alcohol have to do with spiritual things? To understand, you must first realize that you live in a world
filled with unseen beings. The spiritual realm is just as real
as the physical realm that you can see and touch. Wine, or
alcohol, has a nickname: it has traditionally been called *spirits*. In many liquor stores you will still see the sign advertis-
ing "spirits." And these are not good spirits; they're evil,
wicked spirits who plan to overthrow you and your family.

Drinking alcohol makes people helpless—they're less able to protect themselves and their families from threats, both seen and unseen.

And the terrible truth is that most of the unseen world is dark and hostile—you are surrounded by invisible enemies.

READ 1 PETER 5:8:

"Stay alert! Watch out for your great enemy, the devil.
He prowls around like a roaring lion, looking for
someone to devour."

When you drink alcohol, you place yourself under the control of your sin nature and you expose yourself to outright control by the enemy of your soul.

So why did Jesus do this miracle? In the Bible the word *wine* symbolizes or represents joy, celebration, and festivity — and marriage is a very important theme. Remember, this miracle wasn't about whether people should or shouldn't drink wine. Jesus wanted us to notice the wedding.

UNDER the INFLUENCE

LET'S READ EPHESIANS 5:15-20:

"So be careful how you live. Don't live like fools, but like those who are wise. 16 Make the most of every opportunity in these evil days. 17 Don't act thoughtlessly, but understand what the Lord wants you to do.

18 Don't be drunk with wine, because that will ruin your life. Instead, be filled with the Holy Spirit, 19 singing psalms and hymns and spiritual songs among yourselves, and making music to the Lord in your hearts.

20 And give thanks for everything to God the Father in the name of our Lord Jesus Christ."

Keep your bookmark in Ephesians Chapter Five. Notice he says: Don't be drunk with wine, because that will ruin your life. Instead be filled with the Holy Spirit.

Many people have ruined their lives and destroyed their families through drunkenness. But many people have experienced gloriously changed lives when they put themselves under the influence of Christ's Holy Spirit.

Look at verses 19 and 20 again. A life filled with the Spirit of Jesus creates a heart that overflows with thanksgiving and brings joy and healing to you and those around you. In fact, many communities or villages have been changed after just one person placed themselves under the influence and power of the Holy Righteous Spirit of Jesus.

> 43. What behaviors do you expect to see from people who are under the influence of alcohol?
>
> 44. What changes and affects do you expect to see in the life of a person who puts themselves under the influence of God's Holy Spirit?

WAITING for the BRIDEGROOM

Marriage is intended to be a picture of Christ and the church. Believers are called the *bride of Christ*. Therefore, it's fitting that Jesus began His ministry at a wedding. After all, Jesus will finish His ministry at a wedding.

Now return to Ephesians Chapter Five.

"For a husband is the head of his wife as Christ is the head of the church. He is the Savior of his body, the church. 24 As the church submits to Christ, so you wives should submit to your husbands in everything.

25 For husbands, this means love your wives, just as Christ loved the church. He gave up his life for her 26 to make her holy and clean, washed by the cleansing of God's word. 27 He did this to present her to himself as a glorious church without a spot or wrinkle or any other blemish. Instead, she will be holy and without fault.

28 In the same way, husbands ought to love their wives as they love their own bodies. For a man who loves his wife actually shows love for himself. 29 No one hates his own body but feeds and cares for it, just as Christ cares for the church. 30 And we are members of his body.

31 As the Scriptures say, 'A man leaves his father and mother and is joined to his wife, and the two are united into one.' 32 This is a great mystery, but it is an illustration of the way Christ and the church are one."

When this age ends, we will be with Jesus at the marriage supper of the Lamb. There will be a final wedding. And blessed (oh how happy) will those be who are invited and attend the marriage supper of the Lamb!

READ REVELATION 19:6-9:

"Then I heard what seemed to be the voice of a great multitude, like the roar of many waters and like the sound of mighty peals of thunder, crying out, 'Hallelujah! For the Lord our God the Almighty reigns. 7 Let us rejoice and exult and give him the glory, for the marriage of the Lamb has come, and his Bride has made herself ready; 8 it was granted her to clothe herself with fine linen, bright and pure' — for the fine linen is the righteous deeds of the saints.

9 And the angel said to me, 'Write this: Blessed are those who are invited to the marriage supper of the Lamb.' And he said to me, 'These are the true words of God.'"

JESUS SAID IN JOHN 14:1:

"Let not your hearts be troubled. Believe in God; believe also in me. In my Father's house are many rooms. If it were not so, would I have told you that I go to prepare a place for you? And if I go and prepare a place for you, I will come again and will take you to myself, that where I am you may be also."

HOMEWORK:

Continue reading through the books of the New Testament as explained last week. Ask Jesus to explain what you're reading. Ask Him to help you to stay in step with the Holy Spirit and to lead you into all truth.

PRACTICE THESE MEMORY VERSES:

1 Peter 5:8: "Be alert and of sober mind. Your enemy the devil prowls around like a roaring lion looking for someone to devour." NIV

Romans 13:14: ". . . clothe yourselves with the Lord Jesus Christ, and do not think about how to gratify the desires of the flesh." NIV

Ephesians 5:18-20: "Do not get drunk on wine, which leads to debauchery. Instead, be filled with the Spirit, 19 speaking to one another with psalms, hymns, and songs from the Spirit. Sing and make music from your heart to the Lord, 20 always giving thanks to God the Father for everything, in the name of our Lord Jesus Christ." NIV

10

THE TEMPLE
of GOD

We've been studying the Bible
to find Jesus because if we meet Jesus, we
have met God. We've seen that there's only
one God, and He exists in three persons:
God the Father, Jesus the Son, and the Holy
Spirit (who is also called the Spirit of Jesus).

Obviously, God is complicated, and we need
Him to help us to understand these things.
As we've read, Jesus is Almighty, Everlast-
ing God in the flesh—He is the Creator, and
He reveals the Father God to us.

To avoid misunderstandings and guard ourselves against false teachers or false prophets, we're learning to study the whole Bible book by book, slowly and carefully.

We've been studying the book of John verse by verse, letting other scriptures broaden our understanding. We're in John Chapter Two.

READ JOHN 2:13-21:

"It was nearly time for the Jewish Passover celebration, so Jesus went to Jerusalem. 14 In the Temple area he saw merchants selling cattle, sheep, and doves for sacrifices; he also saw dealers at tables exchanging foreign money. 15 Jesus made a whip from some ropes and chased them all out of the Temple. He drove out the sheep and cattle, scattered the money changers' coins over the floor, and turned over their tables.

16 Then, going over to the people who sold doves, he told them, 'Get these things out of here. Stop turning my Father's house into a marketplace!'

17 Then his disciples remembered this prophecy from the Scriptures: 'Passion for God's house will consume me.'

18 But the Jewish leaders demanded, 'What are you doing? If God gave you authority to do this, show us a miraculous sign to prove it.'

19 'All right,' Jesus replied. 'Destroy this temple, and in three days I will raise it up.'

20 'What!' they exclaimed. 'It has taken forty-six years to build this Temple, and you can rebuild it in three days?' 21 But when Jesus said 'this temple,' he meant his own body."

Jesus shows us at least two very important things here:

> One: He is the owner, master, and Lord of the temple of God.
>
> Two: He calls His body a temple.

YOUR BODY is the TEMPLE

READ 1 CORINTHIANS 3:16-17:

"Do you not know that you are a temple of God and that the Spirit of God dwells in you? If any man destroys the temple of God, God will destroy him, for the temple of God is holy, and that is what you are."

If the Spirit of Jesus lives in you, then you are God's temple. God resides in you.

Though you were born with a fallen nature and sinful tendencies, He asks you to give up your former life—die to your old self—and allow Him to remake you, as a new creation. Jesus called this being "born again."

He intends to change you and make you into His holy temple.

119

When Jesus entered the physical temple in Jerusalem, He was angry that it was defiled and full of the wrong things. So He made a whip and cleansed His Father's temple.

Likewise, when the Spirit of Jesus comes into our body, He intends to drive out anything that defiles His temple.

READ 1 CORINTHIANS 6:15-20:

"Do you not know that your bodies are members of Christ? Shall I then take away the members of Christ and make them members of a prostitute? May it never be! Or do you not know that the one who joins himself to a prostitute is one body with her? For He says, 'The two shall become one flesh.' But the one who joins himself to the Lord is one spirit with Him."

UNDER NEW OWNERSHIP (NOT JUST NEW MANAGEMENT)

Jesus died on the cross to pay a penalty for your sins. But He was not paying to buy your sins. He was purchasing *you*.

Because all people are born with a sinful nature (see Galatians 5:19-21), we have all been sold to death and condemnation. In John 8:44 Jesus told the people who were rejecting Him that they belonged to "the devil." Ephesians 2:1 tells us that without Christ, all people are *dead* in their trespasses and sins. Without Christ, we're spiritually dead, slaves to our sinful nature, controlled by the devil, and heirs of condemnation.

Jesus offers to buy you out of your hopeless condition. When you come to the cross, you're agreeing to let Him purchase you with His blood.

If we accept His offer of forgiveness, He becomes our new owner; when He takes possession of His new property, He moves in and begins transforming us into His holy temple.

Acts 20:28 says we are now God's flock, His church, purchased with His own blood.

LET'S READ 2 CORINTHIANS 6:14-18:

"Do not be bound together with unbelievers; for what partnership have righteousness and lawlessness, or what fellowship has light with darkness? Or what harmony has Christ with Belial, or what has a believer in common with an unbeliever? Or what agreement has the temple of God with idols? For we are the temple of the living God; just as God said, 'I will dwell in them and walk among them; And I will be their God, and they shall be My people.'"

When we come to Jesus, we become more than just the people of God. We become the holy temple of God.

45. Who or what do you believe gave Jesus the authority to cleanse the temple in Jerusalem?
46. What gives Jesus the right to cleanse you and your life?

UNDER CONSTRUCTION

When the Spirit of Jesus moves into your body, He makes you into His temple—His holy temple. He wants to get rid of anything that is not supposed to be there.

He wants to clean up your actions, your words, your thoughts, and even your intentions and motives.

READ EPHESIANS 2:19-22:

"So then you are no longer strangers and aliens, but you are fellow citizens with the saints, and are of God's household, having been built on the foundation of the apostles and prophets, Christ Jesus Himself being the corner stone, in whom the whole building, being fitted together, is growing into a holy temple in the Lord."

Jesus comes to us and examines the temple. If necessary, He makes a whip for cleansing. Sometimes this whip looks like trials. It might look like hard times and difficulty. Other times this whip looks like suffering or persecution.

READ ROMANS 5:1-4:

"Therefore, since we have been made right in God's sight by faith, we have peace with God because of what Jesus Christ our Lord has done for us. 2 Because of our faith, Christ has brought us into this place of undeserved privilege where we now stand, and we confidently and joyfully look forward to sharing God's glory. 3 We can rejoice, too, when we run into

problems and trials, for we know that they help us develop endurance. 4 And endurance develops strength of character, and character strengthens our confident hope of salvation."

We're told to rejoice when we face problems and trials—they're for our good; they help us to develop endurance.

We can rejoice when Jesus comes with the whip of trials and suffering. He's purifying His temple and developing His goodness inside of us.

NOW READ VERSES 5-6:

"And this hope will not lead to disappointment. For we know how dearly God loves us, because he has given us the Holy Spirit to fill our hearts with his love. 6 When we were utterly helpless, Christ came at just the right time and died for us sinners."

READ JAMES 1:2-5:

"Dear brothers and sisters, when troubles of any kind come your way, consider it an opportunity for great joy. 3 For you know that when your faith is tested, your endurance has a chance to grow.

4 So let it grow, for when your endurance is fully developed, you will be perfect and complete, needing nothing. 5 If you need wisdom, ask our generous God, and he will give it to you. He will not rebuke you for asking."

Allow Jesus to chase out the money-changers. Let Jesus clean up His temple. Accept hard times with joy and prayer. You are being made holy!

JESUS, MY VERY BEST FRIEND

John 6:44 says that no one can come to Jesus unless the Father draws Him. In fact, we read in Romans 10 verse 20 that God says He was found by people who were not even looking for Him, and He showed Himself to people who were not asking for Him. If we have begun to seek God and look for Jesus, it was all done by God's grace and mercy—and because He desired it.

Since He purchased us with His blood, He owns us. He could be satisfied to simply be our Master. However, He says that He chose us and called us because He wanted us to be *His friends.*

He doesn't just want to own us, or even to have a casual friendship. He wants to be our very best, closest friend ever.

When we find Jesus, we learn that He wants to send His Spirit to live inside of us. He wants to change us so that we are a reflection of Him. He does this by growing His own fruit inside of us, as we allow Him to plant, tend, and harvest His garden.

"But the fruit of the Spirit is love, joy, peace, patience, kindness, goodness, faithfulness, 23 gentleness and self-control. Against such things there is no law."

God is love. This is what love looks like:

Love, joy, peace, patience, kindness, goodness, faithfulness, gentleness, and self-control.

When the Spirit of Jesus is inside of us, He will be growing this fruit—if we allow Him to. Regardless of who we are or where we live, the characteristics of real love are *God's traits*—and they come from Him, only from Him.

47. Have you ever seen changes in yourself because of the influence of certain friends?
48. If you want more love, joy, peace, patience etc. in your life, what steps could you take to achieve that?

LET'S READ JOHN 15:4-5:

"Jesus said, 'Remain in me, as I also remain in you. No branch can bear fruit by itself; it must remain in the vine. Neither can you bear fruit unless you remain in me. 5 I am the vine; you are the branches. If you remain in me and I in you, you will bear much fruit; apart from me you can do nothing.'"

Happiness and joy are the same all over the world. Goodness is the same everywhere, in any language. But this world also has problems. The problems and suffering that men, women, and children have are the same in any country. In any country, sadness feels the same. In any country, we have suffering and trouble.

We all need a friend.

We all need the Spirit of Jesus inside of us to tell us which way to go. We need God's Spirit to heal broken hearts. We need the Spirit of Jesus to set us free from anger, or jealousy, or worry and fear. We need Jesus to feed us, and clothe us, and give us a home.

No matter where we live, we need Jesus. He is the best friend we could ever have. If we will draw near to Him, He will come near to us—to save us and to move inside and transform us into a temple filled with His love.

HOMEWORK:

Continue reading through the books of the New Testament, asking Jesus to help you to understand what you're reading. Begin to set aside a time each day to ask the owner of your body what He wants of you. Ask Him to fill you with His Spirit and to cleanse the temple.

PRACTICE THESE MEMORY VERSES:

1 Corinthians 3:16: "Don't you know that you yourselves are God's temple and that God's Spirit dwells in your midst?" NIV

1 Corinthians 6:19-20: "Do you not know that your bodies are temples of the Holy Spirit, who is in you, whom you have received from God? You are not your own; 20 you were bought at a price. Therefore honor God with your bodies." NIV

2 Corinthians 6:16: "What agreement is there between the temple of God and idols? For we are the temple of the living God. As God has said: "I will live with them and walk among them, and I will be their God, and they will be my people." NIV

11

A NEW HEART

When John the Baptist found Jesus, he called Him the Lamb who takes away the sin of the world. Then the men who became His disciples found Him; they called Him the Messiah, their Lord and their God. When you decided to look for Jesus, you made the best decision in your life. And we've seen that it wasn't entirely your decision; the Father in heaven drew you to Jesus. Now these things will determine whether your search is successful:

a. **where you search:** you cannot look to society to find Jesus; they always create a Jesus

that suits their own lifestyles. You must look
for Jesus in the Bible, which is also called
"God's Word."

b. **why you search:** if you're searching for
your own opinion, idea or desire, you'll miss
the main message of the Scriptures. We must
approach the Scriptures humbly, ready to accept whatever we find.

c. **how you respond when you find Him:**
when you seek Jesus with all of your heart,
you will find Him—but you will find the
bright light of God's law shining on you. You
will see your sinfulness. You will either run
away, or you will repent. If you admit you are
a sinner, and you confess your sins to Jesus, He
will forgive you through His finished work on
the cross.

When you started taking these steps, you began a brand new
life. But you needed Jesus to fill you with His Holy Spirit;
He is the power we need to live this new life.

Now you need His power to change you and cleanse you
so you can continue to walk in His light without shame.

Anytime He shows you your sin, you must repent right
away—ask Jesus to forgive you and to cleanse you and
make you pure.

IT'S a HEART ISSUE

Jesus provides everything we need for life and godliness; He expects us to trust Him with all of our hearts. When we trust Him that much, deeply and from the heart, we are firmly convinced that He knows best and will do what's best with our life, even if appearances say otherwise.

Jesus says that if we try to save ourselves and save our life, we will lose it. But if we give everything to Him, we will gain our life—for eternity.

READ MARK 8:16-17:

"At this they began to argue with each other because they hadn't brought any bread. 17 Jesus knew what they were saying, so he said, 'Why are you arguing about having no bread? Don't you know or understand even yet? Are your hearts too hard to take it in?'"

In this story, the men were worried that their basic needs would not be met. But Jesus rebuked them and said their hearts were hard. Because of their hard hearts, they didn't understand that their Provider was with them. Therefore, they were worried, fighting, and blaming each other.

READ VERSES 18-21:

"Jesus said, 'You have eyes—can't you see? You have ears—can't you hear? Don't you remember anything at all? 19 When I fed the 5,000 with five loaves of bread, how many baskets of leftovers did you pick up afterward?'

'Twelve,' they said.

20 'And when I fed the 4,000 with seven loaves, how many large baskets of leftovers did you pick up?'

'Seven,' they said.

21 'Don't you understand yet?' Jesus asked them."

Naturally speaking, it made sense that the disciples were scared and worried—it appeared they wouldn't have anything to eat. But Jesus was with them! That fact should have changed their outlook. But it didn't—because their hearts were hard. They failed to realize that He was the answer to their problem, so they didn't even ask Him for help. Instead they fought, argued, and blamed each other. Have you ever done this when you were worried?

When our hearts are hard, we don't trust Jesus; we don't really believe that He can, or will, provide for us. We don't expect Jesus to do miracles, so we often forget to ask Him for what we need.

NOW SKIP DOWN, AND READ MARK 8:34-37:

"Then, calling the crowd to join his disciples, he said, 'If any of you wants to be my follower, you must give up your own way, take up your cross, and follow me. 35 If you try to hang on to your life, you will lose it. But if you give up your life for my sake and for the sake of the Good News, you will save it. 36 And what do you benefit if you gain the whole world but lose your own soul? 37 Is anything worth more than your soul?'"

If we try to save our lives, we will lose them. If we fight and argue to get what we need for ourselves, our needs will not be met—and we will ultimately be condemned.

But if we trust Jesus and give everything to Him, we will be saved—and our needs will be met.

If this doesn't make sense, your heart might be hard. Somehow you need to have your heart softened. And Jesus is the answer for that need also!

49. According to Jesus, what type of heart can hinder your understanding?

50. Considering your prayer life and behavior under pressure, what condition do you believe your heart is in?

AN IGNORANT HEART

READ HEBREWS 3:13:

. . . "exhort one another every day, as long as it is called 'today,' that none of you may be hardened by the deceitfulness of sin."

Sin deceives us and makes our hearts grow hard. Even the most intelligent person will progressively lose their ability to understand as their heart grows harder.

READ EPHESIANS 4:18:

"They are darkened in their understanding, alienated from the life of God because of the ignorance that is in them, due to their hardness of heart."

READ MATTHEW 5:8:

"Blessed are the pure in heart, for they shall see God."

If we have a hard heart, our heart is soiled and corrupt, and we cannot see God. But through Jesus Christ we can be born again. In Jesus we can be made into a brand new person with a pure heart—and then we'll be able to see God.

A PURE HEART

God purifies our hearts through faith. Only God can give us a new, clean, soft heart. He gives us this purified heart when we trust in Jesus.

READ ACTS 15:8-9:

"God knows people's hearts, and he confirmed that he accepts Gentiles by giving them the Holy Spirit, just as he did to us. 9 He made no distinction between us and them, for he cleansed their hearts through faith."

"Therefore if anyone is in Christ, he is a new creature; the old things passed away; behold, new things have come."

READ EZEKIEL 36:26:

"The Lord says: 'I will give you a new heart and put a new spirit within you; and I will remove the heart of stone from your flesh and give you a heart of flesh.'"

Only Jesus can make us into a new creation with a new, soft heart. When we cannot see God for who He really is, we often won't take our requests to Him. We don't really trust that He will take good care of us. We need Him to soften and purify our hearts and make us new.

If we are worrying, arguing, and fighting to try and get the things we need, we have a heart problem. We are not trusting Jesus, because our heart is hard.

51. According to Matthew 5:8, what will you see if you have a pure heart?

52. According to Acts 15:9, what did God use to cleanse people's hearts?

HOMEWORK:

Continue reading through the books of the New Testament, asking the Spirit of God to help you to understand what you're reading. Continue setting aside a time each day to ask the owner of your body what He wants of you. Ask Him to soften your heart and help you to trust Him completely. Ask Him to fill you with His Spirit and to purify your heart, so you can see God for who He really is.

PRACTICE THESE MEMORY VERSES:

2 Corinthians 5:17: "Therefore, if anyone is in Christ, that person is a new creation: The old has gone, the new is here!" NIV

Matthew 5:8: "Blessed are the pure in heart, for they will see God." NIV

Ezekiel 36:26: "I will give you a new heart and put a new spirit in you; I will remove from you your heart of stone and give you a heart of flesh." NIV

12

A NEW CREATION

Last week we learned that sin **makes our hearts grow hard.** If we have a hard heart, we cannot understand spiritual things. A hard heart makes us confused and slow to understand.

God offers to give us a new, soft heart—but only when we understand our need and come to Him in faith. However, when we have a hard heart, we are proud—which blinds us to our neediness. If we will ever find Jesus, and if we will ever find life, we desperately need to see our true condition.

"You say, 'I am rich. I have everything I want. I don't need a thing!' And you don't realize that you are wretched and miserable and poor and blind and naked."

NOW READ JOHN 9:39-41:

"Then Jesus told him, 'I entered this world to render judgment—to give sight to the blind and to show those who think they see that they are blind.'

40 Some Pharisees who were standing nearby heard him and asked, 'Are you saying we're blind?'

41 'If you were blind, you wouldn't be guilty,' Jesus replied. 'But you remain guilty because you claim you can see.'"

First we must see and acknowledge our lost condition. Only then will we seek a Savior and a cure.

READ PSALM 51:10:

"Create in me a clean heart, O God, And renew a steadfast spirit within me."

We cannot obtain a soft, pure heart simply by wanting one. Only God can give this gift. And how does He perform this miracle transformation of our heart? By making us into a new creation through our faith in Jesus.

Let's continue studying the book of John verse by verse.

READ JOHN 2:23-25:

**"Because of the miraculous signs Jesus did in Jerusa-
lem at the Passover celebration, many began to trust
in him. 24 But Jesus didn't trust them, because he
knew all about people. 25 No one needed to tell him
about human nature, for he knew what was in each
person's heart."**

Jesus did not trust these people. He knows that all humans
have a spiritual sickness: we're born with evil hearts. When
we sin, we're doing what comes natural. But this sin makes
us blind—we cannot see our true condition. So Jesus didn't
trust Himself to men because He knows that not only are we
born with a sinful core, but we're also blind to this fact.

Since our core is sinful, there's only one cure for what ails us: we must be re-created.

We've just finished John Chapter Two. Now let's begin
Chapter Three.

READ JOHN 3:1-4:

**"There was a man named Nicodemus, a Jewish reli-
gious leader who was a Pharisee. 2 After dark one eve-
ning, he came to speak with Jesus. 'Rabbi,' he said,**

'we all know that God has sent you to teach us. Your miraculous signs are evidence that God is with you.'

3 Jesus replied, 'I tell you the truth, unless you are born again, you cannot see the Kingdom of God.'

4 'What do you mean?' exclaimed Nicodemus. 'How can an old man go back into his mother's womb and be born again?'"

Jesus said the cure for man's spiritual sickness was to become a new person with a new heart. We must all be born *of the Spirit of God.*

KEEP READING VERSES 5-6:

"Jesus replied, 'I assure you, no one can enter the Kingdom of God without being born of water and the Spirit. 6 Humans can reproduce only human life, but the Holy Spirit gives birth to spiritual life.'"

The first time we're born, we are born *of water*. When we trust Jesus, we are born *from His Holy Spirit.* This is our second birth.

53. In John 3:3–5 Jesus told Nicodemus that he could not see the kingdom of God unless what happened?
54. What did the people mentioned in Rev. 3:17 not realize?

BORN ONCE, DIE TWICE; BORN TWICE, DIE ONCE

If you are born only one time, you will die twice. Your body will die, and then you will stand before God. That's the first death.

But then *He who sits on the throne* will say, "Go away, I did not know you. You did not belong to me." And you will be sent into eternal punishment. That is the second death.

But if you're born two times, you will die only once.

If you have been born again, of the Spirit of God, your body will die, and then you will stand in front of God. He will say, "Well done, my good and faithful servant." Then He'll say, "Come in! Enter into my joy. Enter in and live forever!"

If you are born once, you will die twice and spend eternity in hell. If you are born twice, then you will die only one time and spend eternity in paradise.

CONTINUE READING VERSES 7-15:

> "Jesus said, 'So don't be surprised when I say, "You must be born again." 8 The wind blows wherever it wants. Just as you can hear the wind but can't tell where it comes from or where it is going, so you can't explain how people are born of the Spirit.'
>
> 'How are these things possible?' Nicodemus asked.

10 Jesus replied, 'You are a respected Jewish teacher, and yet you don't understand these things? 11 I assure you, we tell you what we know and have seen, and yet you won't believe our testimony. 12 But if you don't believe me when I tell you about earthly things, how can you possibly believe if I tell you about heavenly things?

13 No one has ever gone to heaven and returned. But the Son of Man has come down from heaven. 14 And as Moses lifted up the bronze snake on a pole in the wilderness, so the Son of Man must be lifted up, 15 so that everyone who believes in him will have eternal life.'"

If we are not born again by God's Holy Spirit, our heart is not clean. If we are not born again, we cannot enter heaven, and we cannot see God.

But if we believe on Jesus, our faith cleanses our hearts and we are born again.

NOW READ VERSES 16-18:

"For this is how God loved the world: He gave his one and only Son, so that everyone who believes in him will not perish but have eternal life. 17 God sent his Son into the world not to judge the world, but to save the world through him. 18 There is no judgment against anyone who believes in him. But anyone who does not believe in him has already been judged for not believing in God's one and only Son."

FIND JESUS!

As you study the Bible, remember that there's a safe way and a dangerous way to study. When you hear of the many different, conflicting versions of "Jesus" that this world believes in, you'll see the sad result of seeking Jesus in the wrong places, with the wrong motives, and with the wrong response to His dazzling light.

If you study the Bible safely (book after book, chapter by chapter, verse by verse—allowing the Bible to interpret the Bible for you), you'll learn that there are more false prophets and lying teachers than honest ones. But Jesus never lies; and He said if you continue in His teaching, He'll be sure that you know the truth—and the truth will set you free.

> 55. Since you began studying the Bible, has your opinion of Jesus changed? How has this impacted your life?

LET'S READ 1 TIMOTHY 2:5-6:

"There is one God and one Mediator who can reconcile God and humanity—the man Christ Jesus. He gave His life to purchase freedom for everyone."

In other words, finding Jesus is not optional! Your entire life and your eternity, depend on this.

No matter the cost, you must find Jesus!

I also want you to notice that we have only made it through three chapters (in one book, the book of John), and already we've discovered some very shocking truths:

A. Jesus is God.

B. He is the only way to heaven.

C. You cannot enter heaven naturally. You must be born again, of the Holy Spirit.

READ THESE VERSES ABOUT NEW BIRTH:

1 Peter 1:3: "Blessed be the God and Father of our Lord Jesus Christ, who according to His great mercy has caused us to be born again to a living hope through the resurrection of Jesus Christ from the dead . . . (*now skip down to verse 23*) . . . for you have been born again not of seed which is perishable but imperishable, that is, through the living and enduring word of God."

Galatians 3:26: "For you are all sons of God through faith in Christ Jesus."

Colossians 2:12: . . . . "having been buried with Him in baptism, in which you were also raised up with Him through faith in the working of God, who raised Him from the dead."

Romans 8:9: "However, you are not in the flesh but in the Spirit, if indeed the Spirit of God dwells in you. But if anyone does not have the Spirit of Christ, he does not belong to Him."

If we do not have the Spirit of Jesus inside of us, we do not belong to Him. Jesus wants us to give ourselves to Him, and He wants to give His Spirit to us. If we will give up our old life, He will give us a new life. We will be born again as a new creation. Our sins will be washed away and forgotten. We'll have a new heart and we will have the Spirit of God living inside of us.

After we believe, we must trust that He will do what is best with our life. Human nature is sinful, and we will always have feelings that come from our old nature. But when we are born again, we also have a new nature—the Spirit of Christ—living inside of us. Now we have a choice! We can choose to ignore our own feelings and receive the power that God's Spirit will give us—so we can choose His will over that of our old nature.

When we get scared, we must talk to Jesus. When we are worried, we must talk to Jesus—and trust Him. Give Him your worries. Give Him your fears. Give Him everything.

Finding Jesus means finding that you need Him, and learning to trust Him more than you trust yourself.

As we finish this Bible study, I hope you've been *born again* already. But if you haven't, pray to Jesus now and ask Him to make you into a brand new creation.

By believing what Jesus says and putting your faith in Him, you can be raised up to a new life in the Spirit of God.

"When I saw Him, I fell at His feet as if I were dead. But He laid His right hand on me and said, 'Don't be afraid! I am the First and the Last. I am the living one. I died, but look—I am alive forever and ever! And I hold the keys of death and the grave."

Revelation 1:17-18

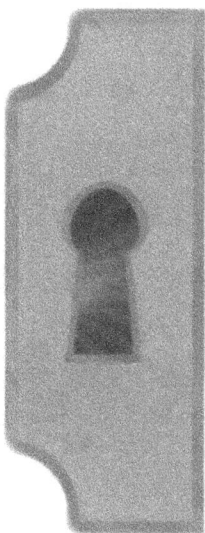

FIND MORE BOOKS LIKE THIS AT:

SWEETWATER STILL PUBLISHING

www.sweetwaterstill.com

SEEK & YOU SHALL FIND

BOOK ONE: FINDING JESUS
BOOK TWO: FINDING TRUTH
BOOK THREE: FINDING HOPE
BOOK FOUR: FINDING POWER

RELATED DISCIPLESHIP RESOURCES:

HIS POWER
LIVING IN STEP WITH THE HOLY SPIRIT
FUNDAMENTALS OF SOUND DOCTRINE

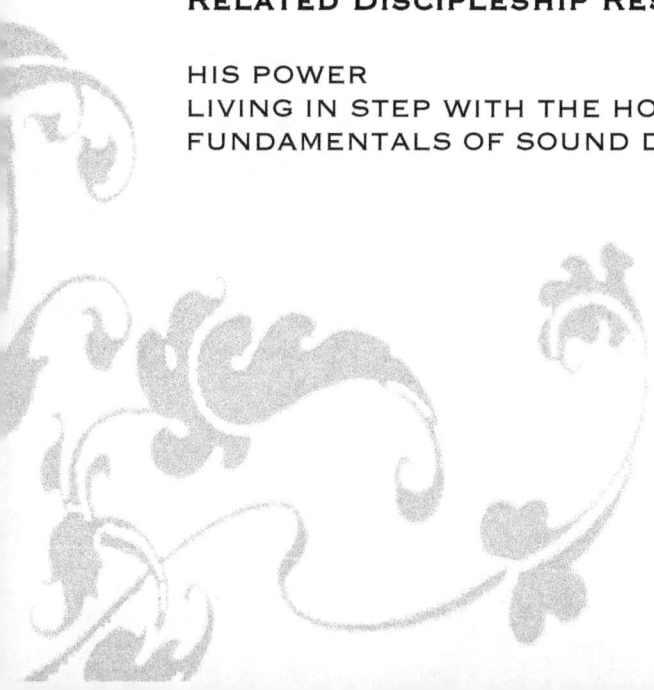

NOTES

We have all sinned.
(See Romans 3:10,23)

The wages of our sins is death.
(See Romans 6:23)

Jesus paid our sin debt on the cross.
(See Romans 5:8)

JESUS IS THE ONLY WAY TO HEAVEN.

"There is salvation in no one else! God has given no other name under heaven by which we must be saved." Acts 4:12

"If we confess our sins, he is faithful and just and will forgive us our sins and purify us from all unrighteousness." 1 John 1:9 NIV

Jesus offers
FORGIVENESS for our sins,
FREEDOM from our sins,
and a NEW PURIFIED LIFE
by the power of His Holy Spirit
inside of us.

Remove this page and share it with someone!

www.ingramcontent.com/pod-product-compliance
Lightning Source LLC
LaVergne TN
LVHW091301080426
835510LV00007B/351